a guide to the
criminal justice system
in england and wales

Foreword

This edition was prepared by Becca Chapman and Stephen Niven of the Crime and Criminal Justice Unit in the Home Office Research, Development and Statistics Directorate, with the assistance of many colleagues in the Home Office, Lord Chancellor's Department and Crown Prosecution Service. The booklet is based on previous editions prepared by Gordon C Barclay. Professor Andrew Ashworth of Oxford University provided a very helpful review in the final stages.

For further information or additional copies, please contact:
RDS Communication and Development Unit
Room 201
50 Queen Anne's Gate
London
SW1H 9AT
United Kingdom

Tel: (020) 7273 2084
Fax: (020) 7222 0211

"The views expressed in this report are those of the authors, not necessarily those of the Home Office (nor do they reflect Government policy)."

The Criminal Justice System - England and Wales
© Crown copyright 2000
    ISBN   1 84082 545 6

Contents

List of figures

1 Introduction

1.1 Purpose

This document provides a description of the structures and procedures of the Criminal Justice System (CJS) in England and Wales. It is intended as a resource for people from a variety of backgrounds and interests. It provides an overview of the whole system rather than a detailed and exhaustive examination of its constituent parts. For a more detailed discussion of the various aspects of the CJS, the Research and Statistics Publications section of this guide lists several references to other more comprehensive accounts. This document is also available on the Internet where there is easy access to related web pages [http://www.homeoffice.gov.uk/rds/cjspub1.html]. This Internet version will be updated more frequently, as and when changes occur. The Criminal Justice System in Scotland is described in 'Crime and Criminal Justice in Scotland'. The Scottish system is independent of that in England and Wales.[1]

1.2 The organisation of the Criminal Justice System

The Criminal Justice System in England and Wales is comprised of several separate agencies and departments which are responsible for various aspects of the work of maintaining law and order and the administration of justice. The main agencies of the CJS include:

- The Police Service
- The Crown Prosecution Service (CPS)
- The Court Service
- Magistrates' courts
- The Crown Court
- The Appeal Courts
- The Prison Service
- The Probation Service
- The Serious Fraud Office
- The Criminal Defence Service
- The Criminal Injuries Compensation Authority
- Other victim and witness care services.

The Home Office, Attorney General's Office and Lord Chancellor's Department are the three main government departments with responsibility for the CJS, providing the policy framework, objectives and targets, funding development and support functions.

---

1. Crime and Criminal Justice in Scotland (1997) Peter Young London: Stationery Office.

Many of these organisations have a long history and a tradition of autonomy and independence. For example, the judiciary remains independent of political influence in their interpretation of the law and their judgements in a particular case. However, they are expected to work within certain frameworks for sentencing, set by legislation and sentence guideline judgements and other Court of Appeal decisions. Similarly the Crown Prosecution Service remain independent in their decision as to whether to prosecute a particular case or not. This independence acts as a check on the system being used for political purposes. It does not necessarily also facilitate a co-ordinated response to the law and order challenges posed by a diverse and changing society. While many of the various agencies and departments which constitute the CJS do have written aims, unlike many other countries there is no criminal or penal 'code' that sets out the principles on which the justice system operates.

A number of joint working initiatives have recently been set up to achieve a greater degree of communication between the agencies and the development of common strategic and operational frameworks (see Chapter 2). Restructuring of the various agencies is in progress so that, at a local level, they will share common geographical boundaries (see Streamlining the Criminal Justice System in Chapter 2).

1.3   Aims and objectives of the Criminal Justice System

In addition to the above, the Government has now set aims for the CJS. The two specific aims and associated objectives provide a strategic direction for the CJS as a whole.

Aim A: To reduce crime and the fear of crime and their social and economic costs.
Objectives:
- to reduce the level of actual crime and disorder
- to reduce the adverse impact of crime and disorder on people's lives
- to reduce the economic costs of crime.

Aim B: To dispense justice fairly and efficiently and to promote confidence in the rule of law.
Objectives:
- to ensure just processes and just and effective outcomes
- to deal with cases throughout the criminal justice process with appropriate speed
- to meet the needs of victims, witnesses and jurors within the system
- to respect the rights of defendants and to treat them fairly
- to promote confidence in the Criminal Justice System.

All the constituent agencies of the CJS have been asked to make sure that their particular aims are integrated with, and complement, these overarching aims. The task is to increase the efficiency and effectiveness of the CJS by encouraging the various participants to work together towards the same aims, while at the same time preserving the autonomy and independence of the various agencies and services. This document provides a brief description of the changes taking place in the CJS and the ways that the various agencies and services perform very specific services and roles.

In order to measure the performance of the system, targets have been set for the aims and objectives of the CJS. These are set out in the CJS Business Plan 2000/2001.

1.4 Resources

Approximately 13 billion pounds will be spent on the CJS in 2000/2001. How this figure is broken down can be seen in Figure 1 below. The chart shows that over half of the money will be spent on the police.

Figure 1.1: Planned spending on the Criminal Justice System in 2000/2001

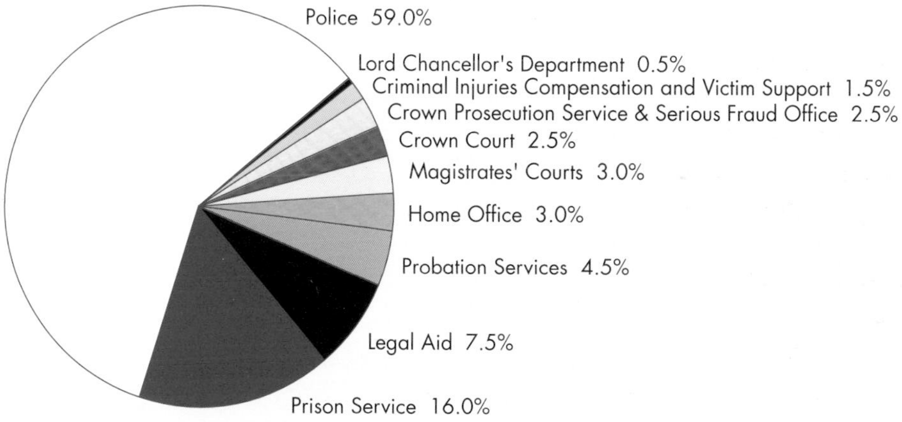

Police 59.0%

Lord Chancellor's Department 0.5%
Criminal Injuries Compensation and Victim Support 1.5%
Crown Prosecution Service & Serious Fraud Office 2.5%
Crown Court 2.5%
Magistrates' Courts 3.0%
Home Office 3.0%
Probation Services 4.5%
Legal Aid 7.5%
Prison Service 16.0%

1.5 The legal system

Figure 2 provides a pictorial representation of the prosecution process of the CJS. (There are various stages at which a case might be stopped, apart from those mentioned in the diagram.)

The system of justice in England and Wales is sometimes referred to as an 'adversarial system' of justice. This is different from an 'inquisitorial' system of justice found in some other countries. In the adversarial system the magistrate(s) or jury decide having heard two opposing presentations of the case. The prosecution and defence parties are free to present their case as they see fit, and to call and examine witnesses as they wish.

Figure 1.2: The prosecution process

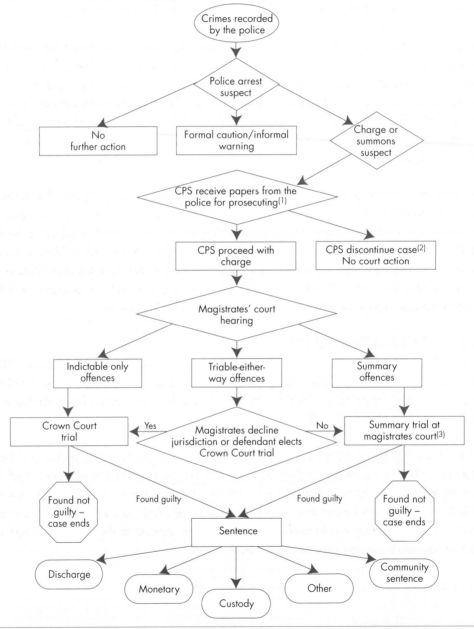

1. Although the majority of prosecutions are handled by the Crown Prosecution Service, other organisations can also bring prosecutions. See section 4.2 for details.
2. A case will be under continued review, and may be discontinued at any stage before the hearing at the magistrates' court or the prosecution may offer no evidence. In addition the charge may be altered up to the final decision of the court.
3. Magistrates may commit to the Crown Court for sentence.

Not guilty pleas result in a contest (hence the term – adversarial) between the two parties arguing over the facts of a case.

In an inquisitorial system a judge is involved in the preparation of evidence by the police and in how the various parties are to present their case at the trial. The judge questions witnesses while prosecution and defence parties can ask supplementary questions. The influence of the judge in the process tends to reduce the level of contest between the two parties. In 1993 a Royal Commission examined the debate over the relative merits of both systems and concluded that, on balance, England and Wales should not move to an inquisitorial system.

Two key tenets of the criminal law in England and Wales are the presumption of innocence, and the standard of proof. The presumption of innocence means that an individual is deemed to be innocent, until proven guilty. The standard of proof required to find a defendant guilty in criminal cases in England and Wales is that the evidence should establish guilt 'beyond reasonable doubt'. This contrasts with the standard of a 'balance of probabilities' used in civil cases, where a person's legal liability is determined if the evidence suggests that the individual is more likely to be guilty than not.

1.6   The Human Rights Act 1998

The UK has been a party to the European Convention for Human Rights (ECHR) since 1951. However, in the past any cases where a citizen wanted to lodge an appeal under the ECHR against a particular ruling or decision have had to be dealt with at the European Court in Strasbourg rather than in the UK courts.

The Human Rights Act 1998, due to be implemented in October 2000, makes it a legal duty for public authorities (including central and local government bodies, courts and the police) to act compatibly with the ECHR, and for all legislation to be interpreted with the ECHR in mind. This will mean that people are able to take their case to the UK courts if they think a public authority has harmed their human rights. Appeal to the European Court will still be possible if the new domestic routes have failed.

The articles in the convention that are made law by the Act are:[2]

Article 2 –   Right to life
Article 3 –   Prohibition of torture

---

2. The articles can be found in more detail in the document 'Putting rights into public service', Home Office Communications Directorate.

Article 4 –   Prohibition of slavery and forced labour

Article 5 –   Right to liberty and security

Article 6 –   Right to a fair trial

Article 7 –   No punishment without law – this article states that no person can be punished for an action which did not constitute a criminal offence at the time it was committed

Article 8 –   Right to respect for private and family life

Article 9 –   Freedom of thought, conscience and religion

Article 10 – Freedom of expression

Article 11 – Freedom of assembly and association

Article 12 – Right to marry

Article 14 – Prohibition of discrimination in the exercise of convention rights

Article 16 – Restrictions on political activity of aliens – this article allows restrictions on the political activities of aliens to be retained

Article 17 – Prohibition of abuse of rights – this article states that nothing in the convention may be used to limit or destroy the freedoms to a greater extent than is provided for in the convention

Article 18 – Limitation on use of restrictions on rights – this article ensures that the restrictions on rights in the convention are not used for any purpose other than those for which they have been prescribed.

First protocol, article 1 –   Protection of property

First protocol, article 2 –   Right to education

First protocol, article 3 –   Right to free elections

Sixth protocol, article 1 –   Abolition of the death penalty

Sixth protocol, article 2 –   Death penalty in time of war – this allows for the use of the death penalty in times of war.

Implementation is a long process as training is necessary for courts and tribunals in dealing with ECHR points, and public authorities need to review legislation and procedures to ensure it complies with ECHR. A Human Rights Task Force has been set up by the Home Office to assist public authorities in preparing for the implementation of the Act. The Task Force also enables a dialogue between the government and the non-governmental organisations covered by the Act.

Once implemented, the Human Rights Act may impact on the Criminal Justice System in a number of ways. All legislation will have to be carefully scrutinised for compatibility with the ECHR. Past court rulings on Human Rights issues must be also be taken into account.

2   Management of the Criminal Justice System

2.1   Government

Three main Government departments share responsibility for criminal justice within England and Wales:

a) The Home Office (HO), which deals with matters relating to criminal law, the police, prisons and probation. The Home Secretary also has general responsibility for internal security.

b) The Lord Chancellor's Department (LCD), which deals with matters relating to the judiciary and administers the Higher Courts (by means of the Court Service). Magistrates' courts are administered through local Committees within a national framework set by the LCD. The Lord Chancellor is head of the judiciary.

c) The Attorney General's Office supervises the Crown Prosecution Service (CPS) which is responsible for the independent prosecution of nearly all criminal cases instituted by the police. It is headed by the Director of Public Prosecutions.

Figure 2.1: The structure of the Criminal Justice System

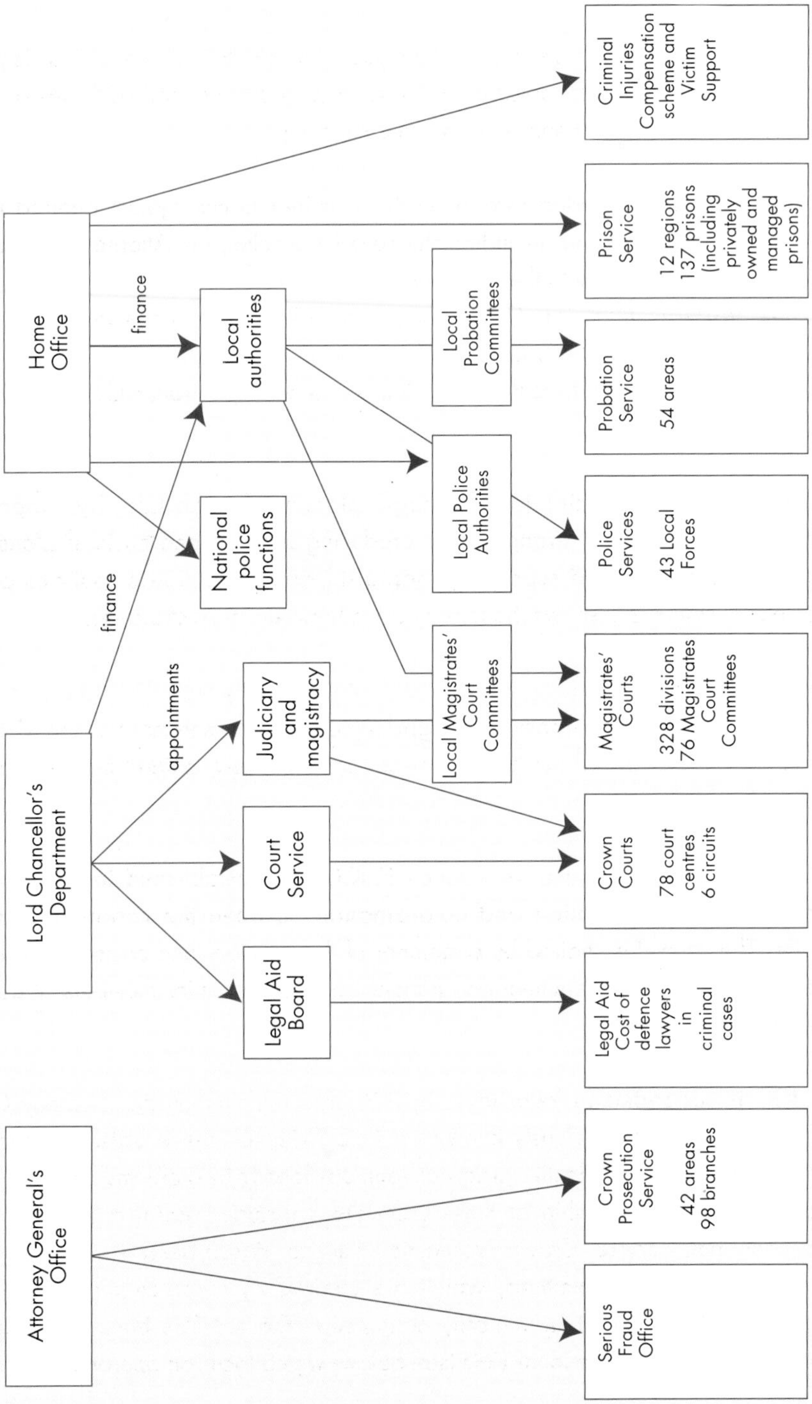

2.2   Cross-agency links

A new approach to administering the CJS began in 1998 with the aim of improving co-operation and co-ordination between the various departments and agencies of the CJS. A new national structure has been set in place comprising:

- A Ministerial Steering Group on the Criminal Justice System chaired by the Home Secretary and including the Lord Chancellor, the Attorney General and the Chief Secretary to the Treasury
- A Strategic Planning Group of senior officials from the three main CJS departments and the Treasury
- A Criminal Justice Joint Planning Unit comprising staff from HO, LCD, CPS and the Treasury.

The new structure maintains joint strategic planning for the CJS, by supporting joint performance management arrangements; producing strategic and business plans; reporting annually on progress; and supporting appraisal and evaluation of policies on a "what works" basis. Figure 2.2 shows the relationships between these structures.

A cross-departmental Integrating Business and Information Systems (IBIS) Group is in place to maximise benefits from information and business systems across the CJS. A work programme will be carried out by a cross-departmental unit, guided by a board of senior officials.

The Criminal Justice Consultative Council (CJCC) was established in 1992 to improve communication, co-operation and co-ordination between the various criminal justice agencies. The council is chaired by a member of the judiciary and comprises members from all the criminal justice government departments, as well as senior members of each agency and legal professions.

The CJCC is supported at local level by 42 Area Criminal Justice Strategy Committees (ACJSCs). These were previously known as Area Criminal Justice Liaison Committees. The role of the ACJSCs is to identify practical solutions locally to problems affecting more than one agency. The membership of these committees includes senior representatives of the police, Probation Service, Crown Prosecution Service, Prison Service, magistrates and the legal profession. The committees, which are chaired by a senior judge, also include a representative from the ethnic minority community. The ACJSCs have a strategic role to complement the work of the local TIGs (see below) which focus on operational issues.

Figure 2.2: Management of the Criminal Justice System

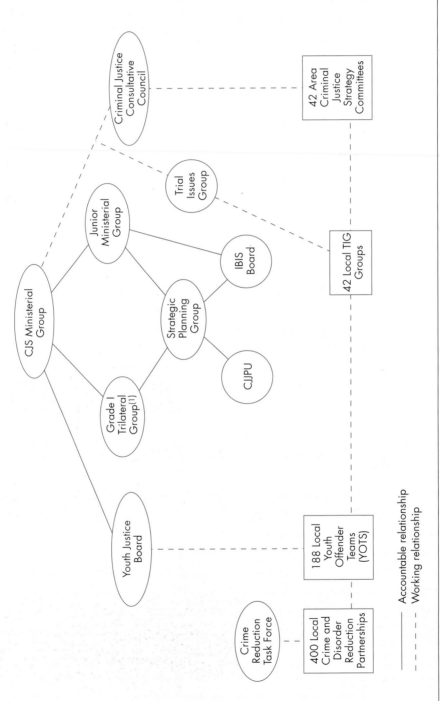

Criminal Justice Consultative Council

42 Area Criminal Justice Strategy Committees

Trial Issues Group

Junior Ministerial Group

IBIS Board

CJS Ministerial Group

Strategic Planning Group

42 Local TIG Groups

CJPU

Grade I Trilateral Group(1)

Youth Justice Board

188 Local Youth Offender Teams (YOTS)

Crime Reduction Task Force

400 Local Crime and Disorder Reduction Partnerships

——— Accountable relationship

– – – Working relationship

1. Departmental Permanent Secretaries' forum ensuring that the three criminal justice departments operate collectively and develop consistent policies, wherever necessary.

The Trial Issues Group (TIG) brings together representatives of all those working in the Criminal Justice System to iron out inter-agency difficulties and to improve the working of the system generally. It has existed since 1990, when it was known as the Working Group on Pre-Trial Issues. The group focuses on practical and operational matters, and has been involved in national work through its sub-groups:

- The Reducing Delays subgroup is responsible for overseeing the implementation of proposals from the 'Narey' report (see 4.3)
- The Joint Performance Management Strategy Group encourages agencies to work together to improve performance
- The Witness Care subgroup has established a Statement of National Standards for Witness Care
- The Manual of Guidance Editorial Board provides guidelines for the preparation, processing and submission of prosecution files
- The Case Management Working Group has recently made a number of recommendations for improvement in the operation of the Crown Court.

Local Trial Issues Groups have been established in each of the 42 criminal justice areas. The core membership of local TIGs includes representatives of all the various CJS agencies and services, with sufficient operational experience, who are also in a position within their organisations to influence and implement new practice and procedure. Chairmanship of local TIGs is determined locally; many are chaired by experienced representatives of the CPS and police who retain an operational role. The Terms of Reference of the local TIGs reflect the aims and objectives for the CJS as a whole, and encourage a close relationship with the local Area Criminal Justice Strategy Committees (see above).

Crime and Disorder Reduction Partnerships have been set up following the Crime and Disorder Act 1998. These partnerships are supported by the Crime Reduction Task Force. Crime reduction is discussed in further detail in Chapter 7.

The Crime and Disorder Act 1998 established the Youth Justice Board for England and Wales as a Home Office sponsored non-departmental public body to monitor and co-ordinate the delivery of youth justice services for young people (10- to 17- year-olds) in England and Wales. The same Act also established Youth Offending Teams (YOTS) which are multi-agency groups implementing and co-ordinating youth justice services at a local level. Both these developments are described in more detail in Chapter 5.

There are a number of inspectorates working within the CJS, assessing the performance of different agencies. These inspectorates are beginning to co-operate together in joint inspections and new programmes of work. This includes a joint study on CJS casework information needs that was published in April 2000, and proposals for a new unit to co-ordinate cross-agency inspections and thematic reviews.

2.3   Streamlining the Criminal Justice System across 42 areas

The Government is aligning the geographical boundaries of the different agencies and services in the CJS so that it is easier for agencies to work effectively at local level to address common issues, co-ordinate effort and achieve outcomes across organisational boundaries.

Ministers have agreed that the 42 local police force areas (counting the City of London and Metropolitan Police as one) be adopted to determine the local boundaries for the CJS. The Metropolitan Police District boundaries have also been aligned with the outer boundary of the London Boroughs. On 1 April 1999, the Crown Prosecution Service restructured into 42 areas, consistent with police force areas. The Prison Service has moved to a new 13 area structure which aligns more closely with the 42 area boundaries. Future plans include:

- proposals to reduce the number of Probation Service Areas from 54 to 42 in line with the 42 police force areas, while maintaining an element of regional management at a level equivalent to the 10 Government Offices for the Regions
- amalgamation of the Magistrates' Courts Committee areas. The process of reducing the number of areas from 96 to 42 is expected to be completed by April 2001
- changing the boundaries that affect the Crown Court so that they align with one or more of the 42 areas.

2.4   European Union

The European Union has not in the past been seen to be involved in criminal justice issues, leaving such matters to organisations such as the Council of Europe and the United Nations. However, Article 29 of the Treaty on European Union states that the Union has the objective to establish an area of freedom, security and justice by preventing and fighting against criminality. Over recent years a programme has been developed on organised crime and police co-operation on drugs. A meeting of the European Council in December 1999 in Tampere (Finland) put future priorities on the prevention of urban crime, especially juvenile delinquency and drug-related crime, and the development of police co-operation and exchange of experience.

3   Organisation of the Criminal Justice System

3.1   The Police Service

3.1.1   *Origins*

The first centrally controlled police force in England and Wales emerged in London in 1829, as a result of the Metropolitan Police Improvement Act introduced by Sir Robert Peel. Prior to this, ad hoc arrangements existed in different areas, with watchmen and constables employed by boroughs. Following the setting up of the Metropolitan Police, forces followed in other cities and counties. The early police forces concentrated mainly on patrolling the streets.

The Police Act 1964 began a significant reorganisation of the structure of policing in England and Wales, including a reduction in the number of forces. In 1966 the number of forces outside London was reduced from 117 to 49, and then, under the Local Government Act 1972, to 41.

The 1964 Act also redefined the functions and responsibilities of the Home Secretary, local Police Authorities and Chief Constables in relation to police forces. Under this 'tripartite' system, Chief Constables were given 'direction and control' of their forces, Police Authorities were responsible for maintaining an 'adequate and efficient' police force and the Home Secretary had a variety of supervisory and co-ordinating functions, including the promotion of police efficiency. From the early 1980s the efficiency and effectiveness of policing became major concerns. New management systems were developed and business principles incorporated.

Following a period in which the police experienced difficulties, concerns about the standards of public service grew, and the idea of a police 'service' rather than a police 'force' developed. The 'Statement of Common Purpose and Values' was issued in 1990, re-stating the police service's commitment to serving the needs of the public and adopting a more 'customer' oriented approach to policing.

Specialist functions emerged as the police service grew. One of the most recent of these is the development of the National Criminal Intelligence Service (NCIS). This service has five regional offices dedicated to developing tactical intelligence to fight the most sophisticated crimes. The NCIS was set up in 1991, and was defined in detail and made independent of central government by the Police Act 1997.

3.1.2 Organisation

Each of the regular police forces in England and Wales is maintained by a police authority. Outside London, the authorities comprise local councillors and magistrates; under the provisions of the Police and Magistrates' Courts Act 1994, the police authorities also include independent members. In London, prior to July 2000, the authority for the Metropolitan Police Service (MPS) was the Home Secretary. However, the Greater London Authority Act 1999 established a new police authority for London, the Metropolitan Police Authority (MPA). The new London authority comprises 12 members from the new London Assembly, four magistrates and seven independent members. The authority for the City of London Police is a committee of the Corporation of London and includes councillors and magistrate members.

Police authorities are financed by central government grants and a precept on the council tax. Subject to the approval of the Home Secretary and to regulations, police authorities appoint the Chief Constable. In England and Wales, Chief Constables are responsible for publishing annual policing plans and annual reports, setting local objectives, setting the budget and levying the precept. The Home Secretary is responsible for the organisation, administration and operation of the police service. This role includes making regulations covering such matters as police rank, discipline, hours of duty and pay and allowances.

All police forces are subject to inspection by HM Inspectors of Constabulary (HMIC), who report to the Home Secretary, and whose reports are published. For well over a century HMIC has been charged with examining and improving the efficiency of the police service in England and Wales. In addition, the Home Secretary lays before Parliament a clear statement of the duties and responsibilities which the Inspectorate is expected to fulfil. Inspectors of Constabulary are appointed by the Crown on the recommendation of the Secretary of State.

Offences committed on trains or at stations are handled by the British Transport Police. The Ministry of Defence (MoD) Police handles MoD establishments. In addition, there are a number of forces, such as the Royal Parks Police, whose officers have defined territorial powers.

The Stephen Lawrence Inquiry

In February 1999, Sir William Macpherson published a report: 'The Stephen Lawrence Inquiry'. This was almost six years after the racist murder of Stephen Lawrence, for which no one had been convicted. The report concluded that the Metropolitan Police Service made fundamental errors in the investigation of this case partly as a result of institutional racism. The report defined institutional racism as "the collective failure of an organisation to provide an appropriate and professional service to people because of their colour, culture or ethnic origin". It also defined a racist incident as "any incident which is perceived to be racist by the victim or any other person". The report made a number of recommendations for change in all the police services in order to eliminate institutional racism and to "increase trust and confidence in policing amongst ethnic minority communities". This report will have ongoing implications for the police and their relationship with the communities they serve.

3.1.3   The Special Constabulary

Each police force also has a Special Constabulary, a part-time volunteer force. Special constables have full police powers within their force area and undertake regular officers' routine policing duties when required, thus freeing regulars at times of emergency for other tasks. There were 16,484 special constables in post at the end of March 1999.[3]

---

3.   Police Service Personnel: England and Wales as at 31 March 1999. Home Office Statistical Bulletin 14/99.

3.2   Crown Prosecution Service

3.2.1   *Origins*

Prior to the creation of the CPS in 1985, the police and Director of Public Prosecutions were responsible for the prosecution of criminal cases. A Royal Commission on Criminal Procedure concluded in 1981 that there was a need for an agency independent of the police to conduct prosecutions and encourage consistency and independence in prosecution. The Crown Prosecution Service was thus set up as a single independent and nationwide authority for England and Wales[4] with responsibility for:

- giving pre-charge advice to the police
- reviewing all cases and deciding whether to proceed
- overseeing the progress of cases
- conducting the prosecution of cases in the magistrates' courts
- instructing counsel in the Crown Court.

3.2.2   *Organisation and Role*

The aim of the CPS is to 'contribute to the reduction of both crime and the fear of crime and to increase public confidence in the criminal justice system, by fair and independent review of cases and by firm, fair and effective presentation at court'.

The objectives supporting this Aim are:

- to deal with prosecution cases in a timely and efficient manner in partnership with other agencies
- to ensure that the charges proceeded with are appropriate to the evidence and to the seriousness of the offending by the consistent, fair and independent review of cases in accordance with the Code for Crown Prosecutors
- to enable the courts to reach just decisions by fairly, thoroughly and firmly presenting prosecution cases, rigorously testing defence cases and scrupulously complying with the duties of disclosure
- to meet the needs of victims and witnesses in the Criminal Justice System, in co-operation with the other criminal agencies

The CPS is under a statutory duty to take over the conduct of criminal proceedings from the police (save for certain minor traffic offences). Each case that the police send to the CPS is reviewed to make sure that it meets the tests set out in the Code for Crown Prosecutors. If

---

4.   Prosecution of Offences Act 1985, Chapter 23.

there is insufficient evidence to provide a realistic prospect of conviction or it is considered that a prosecution is not in the public interest, the CPS has the authority to discontinue or otherwise terminate the proceedings.

In April 1999, following the Glidewell Review, the Crown Prosecution Service was re-organised from 14 into 42 areas to align with the 42 area structure of the Criminal Justice System. Within each area there are one or more local branches headed by a Branch Crown Prosecutor responsible for teams of lawyers and caseworkers.

Each area has its own Chief Crown Prosecutor (CCP) who manages a team of lawyers and caseworkers. They report to the Director of Public Prosecutions but remain accountable to the local community for their performance. The CCP is also responsible for developing relationships with the Chief Constable and other agencies in the criminal justice system. Lawyers and caseworkers will be based at joint CPS/police criminal justice units to service the magistrates' courts or at Trial Units to concentrate on the preparation of the more serious casework at the Crown Court. National rollout for these new arrangements began in April 2000.

The CPS Inspectorate, established in 1996, conducts inspections in each CPS area to promote the efficiency and effectiveness of the Crown Prosecution Service through a process of inspection and evaluation; the provision of advice; and the identification and promotion of good practice. The CPS Inspectorate will become an independent body during 2000, and will inspect and report on the CPS as a whole, covering all aspects of performance including inter-agency co-operation, diversity and resource management.

3.3   The Serious Fraud Office

The Serious Fraud Office (SFO) was established in 1988, following the 1986 Fraud Trials Committee Report (the Roskill Report). Its role is to investigate and prosecute cases of serious or complex fraud and therefore contribute to deterring such fraud. It is an independent government department operating, like the CPS, under the superintendence of the Attorney General. The creation of the SFO introduced a multi-disciplinary approach to the investigation and prosecution of serious fraud. Each case is allocated to a team that includes lawyers, financial investigators, information technology and other specialists, law clerks and police officers, of whom there are a substantial number working on the SFO cases at any one time. The SFO makes extensive use of outside expertise, using private sector accountants to assist in investigations and counsel to prosecute. All SFO cases are large, and are normally transferred direct to the Crown Court (see 4.6).

3.4   Courts

3.4.1   Origins

The present legal system in England and Wales has its origins in the 12th century expansion of institutions that were established following the conquest of England by the Normans in 1066. Before that time, there were some differences between the criminal justice procedures in the different counties of England. Unlike the rest of Europe, where legal systems were based on Roman law, England developed what was known as the system of English common law. The centralisation of the system, combined with the residual need for local investigation and trial, led to the development of the major court of common law (the 'assizes'). It was not until 1972, when the Crown Court was introduced, that these institutions were finally abolished. The Court of Appeal was established in 1907 by the Criminal Appeal Act, introducing rights of appeal for defendants in indictable cases.

Although lay magistrates have existed since the 12th century, it was not until 1849 that the Petty Sessions, at which they had presided over matters of summary jurisdiction since the 16th century, were recognised as courts by law.[5] These developed into the magistrates' courts of today.

Within Wales, a separate legal system had evolved and even after the invasion of Wales in 1304, no attempt was made to substitute English for Welsh law. It was not until 1535 that Wales was finally incorporated into the common law framework. In Scotland, a system based upon Roman law developed. Following the merger of the Parliaments of Scotland and England and Wales in 1707, no attempt was made to unite the two systems and so they remain distinct today and develop side by side. The position remains essentially the same despite the constitutional changes of 1999. In Wales, the new Welsh Assembly has no jurisdiction over crime and justice affairs. In Scotland, the new parliament has jurisdiction over crime and justice affairs and the Scottish legal system will continue to be distinct.

3.4.2   Organisation and role

Approximately ninety-six per cent of criminal cases are dealt with summarily at a *magistrates' court*. The case may be tried either by at least two but usually three lay magistrates or by a District Judge (Magistrates' Courts), who will usually sit alone. Until August 2000 these District Judges were known as Stipendiary magistrates, but were renamed in order to recognise them as members of the professional judiciary, as they are legally qualified and salaried.[6] Lay magistrates are appointed by the Crown (retiring at the

---

5. The Petty Sessions Act 1849.
6. Following the expected implementation of s.78 of the Access to Justice Act 1999.

age of 70). They are not paid but may claim expenses and an allowance for loss of earnings. They come from all walks of life and do not usually have any legal qualifications. They are advised on the law by qualified clerks. Magistrates cannot normally order sentences of imprisonment which exceed 6 months (or 12 months for consecutive sentences) or fines exceeding £5,000. In triable-either-way cases (see Chapter 4) the offender may be committed by the magistrates to the Crown Court if a more severe sentence is thought necessary.

Magistrates' courts are locally managed by independent Magistrates' Courts Committees, accountable to the Lord Chancellor. As at 1st April 2000, the magistrates' courts in England and Wales were divided in into 328 independent Petty Sessional Areas, and administered locally by Magistrates' Courts Committees.

Certain magistrates' courts are designated as *Youth Courts*. Such a court is composed of specially trained justices and deals only with charges against and applications relating to children and young persons aged under 18. It sits apart from other courts and, unlike other courts, is not open to the public. It consists of not more than three justices, including at least one man and one woman.

On 1 January 1972 following the Courts Act, the courts of Assize and Quarter Sessions were replaced by a single *Crown Court* with power to sit anywhere in England and Wales. It is part of the Supreme Court. The Court has jurisdiction to deal with all trials on indictment and with persons committed for sentence, and to hear appeals from lower courts, including youth cases. The Act imposed no geographical limitations on the catchment area of Crown Court centres. This means that county and district boundaries have no statutory significance in determining where a case should be heard. Although most Crown Court cases are heard at the centre most convenient to the magistrates' court which committed the case for trial, some types of offence are directed to certain court tiers, for example, a homicide or rape offence. The more serious offences can be tried only by a High Court judge, others may be dealt with by a circuit judge or recorder. There are currently 78 main Crown Court centres divided into six regions, known as Circuits. It is intended for these to be realigned with one or more of the 42 criminal justice areas (see 2.3).

The Court Service became an executive agency of the Lord Chancellor's Department on 3 April 1995. From that date, the administration of the Crown Court became the responsibility of the Court Service. Responsibility for policy issues of the criminal courts and judicial appointments remain with the Lord Chancellor's Department.

Figure 3.1: **The structure of the criminal court in England and Wales**

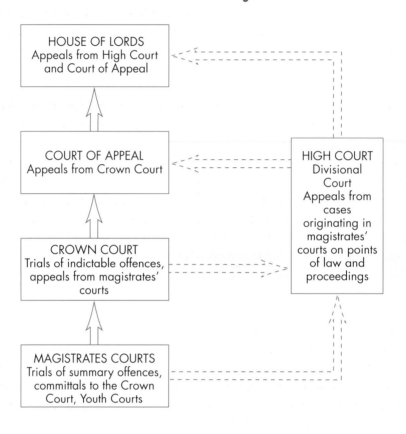

Figure 3.1 presents the basic structures of the criminal courts and ignores the considerable workload of these courts regarding civil and family matters. It also greatly simplifies the relationships between the courts and should not be read as a comprehensive statement on the various responsibilities of the criminal courts.

The Supreme Court consists of the Court of Appeal, the High Court and the Crown Court. A person convicted at a magistrates' court may appeal to the Crown Court, while a person convicted at the Crown Court may appeal to the Court of Appeal and finally to the House of Lords. Appeals on points of law and proceedings arising in the magistrates' courts are dealt with by the Queen's Bench, Divisional Court of the High Court. It has very limited jurisdiction in such matters arising in the Crown Court. The highest court in the land is the House of Lords. This court is composed of the Lords of Appeal, who are lawyers of eminence generally appointed from amongst the judges of the Court of Appeal. They deal with points of law of general public importance brought before them on appeal from the Supreme Court.

A Magistrates' Courts Service Inspectorate was established in January 1993 and placed on a statutory footing by the Police and Magistrates' Courts Act 1994. Its purpose is to inspect the administration and management of the magistrates' court service, in order to improve performance and disseminate good practice.

The Criminal Courts Review

At the end of 1999, the Lord Chancellor appointed Lord Justice Auld to conduct a wide ranging, independent Review of the Criminal Courts in England and Wales. The Terms of Reference for this Review are:

'A review into the practices and procedures of, and the rules of evidence applied by, the criminal courts at every level, with a view to ensuring that they deliver justice fairly, by streamlining all their processes, increasing their efficiency and strengthening the effectiveness of their relationships with others across the whole of the criminal justice system, and having regard to the interests of all parties including victims and witnesses, thereby promoting public confidence in the rule of law.'

The Review is due to report by the end of 2000.

3.4.3   Sentencing Advisory Panel

The Sentencing Advisory Panel is an advisory and consultative non-departmental public body established under the Crime and Disorder Act 1998 and sponsored by the Home Office and the Lord Chancellor's Department. Its function is to provide advice to the Court of Appeal to assist the Court in framing sentencing guidelines. The guidelines of the Court of Appeal are a part of case law and the lower courts have regard to them when passing sentence. When the Court of Appeal plans to make guidelines on an offence or a particular group of offences, it will alert the Panel and the Panel will provide views. Advice is prepared after consultation with a wide range of organisations and consideration of statistical and research evidence. The panel can take the initiative in proposing guidelines, or it can be asked to provide guidelines by the Court of Appeal, or the Home Secretary.

3.5   The Probation Service

3.5.1   Origins

The predecessors of modern probation officers were late 19th century church workers who agreed to be responsible for juvenile offenders, in order to save them from prison. The Probation of Offenders Act 1907 enabled courts to appoint probation officers to advise, assist and befriend offenders. The Probation Service has since developed into a law enforcement agency responsible for advising the court on suitable sentences through pre-sentence reports, and for supervising offenders in the community. The principal purposes of the service are to protect the public, to reduce reoffending and to secure the proper punishment and rehabilitation of offenders

3.5.2   Organisation and role

There are 54 probation areas in England and Wales each under the authority of a probation committee. The probation committee must appoint a Chief Probation Officer who is responsible for the efficient and effective use of resources in the area. The majority of these committees include justices drawn from the local magistrates' courts, but persons are co-opted from other fields as well. It is planned that by April 2001 these 54 autonomous areas will be replaced by a unified National Probation Service, comprising 42 larger areas and aligning with the 42 police authorities. They will be under the control of a National Director who will be directly accountable to the Home Secretary.

Probation staff carry out a number of roles, including the supervision of community penalties imposed on adult offenders. These include penalties such as probation, community service and combination orders as well as supervision orders for offenders aged 10 to 17. Offenders who are 16 or over may also be subject to curfew orders with electronic monitoring, which may be served in conjunction with other community penalties (see Chapter 4). Probation staff are responsible for carrying out assessments on offenders to ascertain their suitability for electronic monitoring. These assessments can be in the form of a specific sentence report (SSR) or as a part of a more general pre-sentence report (PSR) (for more discussion on SSRs and PSRs see 4.10). However, probation officers are not responsible for monitoring compliance with the curfew.

Under the provisions of the Criminal Justice Act 1991, young offenders and adults sentenced to 12 months or more in custody are supervised by the Probation Service before and after release. Since January 1999 an increasing number of these offenders have been released early to spend up to 60 days electronically monitored in the community under the Home Detention Curfew scheme (see Chapter 4). Probation staff, in collaboration with prison staff, are responsible for assessing prisoners' suitability for early release under this system.

HM Inspectorate of Probation, a departmental inspectorate within the Home Office, examines and reports on the performance of area probation services. Its aims are to:

- assess the extent to which probation areas are providing high quality advice to the criminal and civil courts and contributing to public protection by the effective supervision of offenders

- assess whether the services delivered represent value for money
- report their findings, including recommendations for improvement.

National standards covering the main areas of the Probation Service work were revised in December 1999 to come into force from 1 April 2000. Over 600 (9%) probation officers are seconded to Prison Service establishments,[7] where they work alongside prison officers and other specialists to confront offending behaviour and to maintain continuity between the custodial and community parts of the sentence.

3.6   The Prison Service

3.6.1   Origins

Prisons in their present form have existed for about 200 years. Prior to this, execution or transportation to the colonies were the main punishments for serious offences and the few prisons that did exist were used to hold debtors or people awaiting trial. In 1777, John Howard published 'The State of the Prisons', a critical review of the conditions of prisons. This, in combination with the decline in the use of transportation, led to a change in the

---

7. Probation Statistics: England and Wales 1998. Home Office January 2000.

function and conditions of prisons. The Penitentiary Act 1779 gave prisons the task of transforming criminals into law-abiding citizens. Within 50 years, prisons became the main mode of punishment used by criminal courts in Britain. Since then governments have become increasingly involved in the administration of prisons. Prisons were owned and managed by local authorities until the 1877 Prison Act brought all prisons under central government control. In 1963, the Prison Commission was abolished, and prisons were managed directly by the Home Office until 1993 when the modern Prison Service evolved. As a result of provision in the Criminal Justice Act 1991, the management of prisons can now be contracted out to the private sector. By 2000 there were seven privately managed prisons in England and Wales.

3.6.2   Organisation and role

There are 137 Prison Service establishments in England and Wales. These include high security prisons, local prisons, closed and open training prisons, young offender institutions (for sentenced prisoners under the age of 21) and remand centres. All adult male prisoners are placed into one of four security categories A,B, C or D. Category A prisoners are those whose escape would be highly dangerous to the public or to the security of the State. Category B prisoners do not demand the highest level of security but still pose a risk. Category C prisoners are those judged to have neither the will nor the resources to make a determined escape. Prisons holding category A to C prisoners are termed 'Closed' prisons. Category D or 'Open' prisons hold prisoners who do not pose a risk and who are not likely to try to escape. Women and young offenders may be placed in Category A establishments but are not categorised otherwise. They may be held in open or closed prisons depending on risk.

The Prison Service is currently transforming its management and care of juveniles. In 2000-2001 a new separate juvenile prison 'estate', managed separately from the adult facilities will be introduced. The Youth Justice Board will have responsibility for purchasing places in this system. The new estate will involve a new regime of tailored programmes for confronting drug abuse, offending behaviour, lack of educational skills and employment prospects.

The Service's Statement of Purpose is:
> "Her Majesty's Prison Service serves the public by keeping in custody those committed by the courts. Our duty is to look after them with humanity and help them lead law-abiding and useful lives in custody and after release."

Accordingly, the Prison Service has committed itself to two objectives.

- Protect the public by holding those committed by the courts in a safe, decent and healthy environment
- Reduce crime by providing constructive regimes which address offending behaviour, improve educational and work skills and promote law abiding behaviour in custody and after release.

All prisons, remand centres and young offender institutions holding men, women and young people in England and Wales are subject to inspection, whether they are managed directly by the Prison Service or contracted out. The Inspectorate undertakes about 20 full inspections each year.

The Home Secretary appoints the Prisons Ombudsman to hear the complaints of prisoners that were not resolved using internal procedures. The Prisons Ombudsman submits annual reports to the Home Secretary and can also make recommendations in response to particular complaints.

The prison population in England and Wales at the end of March 2000 was 65,460, two per cent higher than at the end of March 1999 (64,210). If custody rates and sentence lengths remain at these levels, the prison population will be 70,400 in 2007.[8]

---

8. Projections of long term trends in the prison population to 2007. Home Office Statistics Bulletin 2/00.

4   Procedures within the Criminal Justice System

4.1   Detection and charging

Every year just under two million people are arrested by the police. A study conducted in 1993–4 found that in three-quarters of cases, arrests were made as a result of a reaction to information – e.g. from the public or through the force control room.[9] Twenty four per cent of arrests were the result of 'proactive' policing – either as a result of surveillance or enquiries, or in half of these cases, as a result of stop and search procedures.

Prior to the Police and Criminal Evidence Act 1984 (PACE), stop and search powers varied across the country, and procedures differed between forces and were often unclear. PACE introduced a general power to stop and search persons or vehicles for stolen or prohibited articles, if officers had reasonable suspicion that they might be present. PACE also introduced safeguards into the procedure involving the provision of information to the suspect about the reasons for suspicion. Around one in eight searches lead to an arrest. Some problems with stop and search remain. The higher rates of stop and search for black persons compared with white or Asian were highlighted by the Macpherson report (see 3.1.2). Although the report suggested no change in current legislation it did recommend the systematic recording of stops (currently only searches are recorded) carried out under any legislation (not just PACE), and of non-statutory or so called 'voluntary' stops. The recording of such stops is now being piloted.

Around 55 per cent of suspects admit to offences after being arrested by the police.[10] Securing a confession is an important aim of interviewing suspects. Interviews with suspects are usually audio-taped, although this is only legally required if the offence in question is indictable or triable-either-way (see 3.4). Some terrorist and Official Secrets Act offences are exempt from tape recording. The custody officer may also authorise a non-recorded interview if the necessary equipment or facilities are not available.[11] The rules governing the right to silence were altered in 1994 to allow courts to draw inferences from a suspect's failure to mention facts at an initial interview which they later rely on as a defence in court.[12]

---

9.   Entry into the criminal justice system: a survey of police arrests and their outcomes. Home Office Research Study No. 185.
10. Entry into the criminal justice system: a survey of police arrests and their outcomes. Op cit.
11. Police and Criminal Evidence Act 1984, Code E.
12. Criminal Justice and Public Order Act 1994.

Prior to this change, about ten per cent of suspects interviewed refused to answer any questions put to them, compared with six per cent after the revision in the rules.[13]

Following the identification of a suspect for an offence, the options open to the police are as follows.

No further action

The police may decide to take no action because they consider there is insufficient evidence to prosecute or that an informal warning may be sufficient. No further action will also be taken when the suspect is a child under ten years, and therefore below the age of criminal responsibility.

Caution

A caution can be given when there is sufficient evidence for a conviction and it is not considered to be in the public interest to institute criminal proceedings. Additionally, the offender must admit guilt and consent to a caution in order for one to be given. A formal caution may be given by, or on the instructions of, a senior police officer. Cautions have traditionally been most used for juvenile and first time offenders. A system of reprimands and final warnings replaced cautioning for juveniles in June 2000. See Chapter 5 for further details.

Fixed penalties

The police may issue a fixed penalty notice for a wide range of motoring offences. Unpaid notices are registered as a fine by magistrates' courts without any court appearance being necessary. The court will then pursue payment of the amount in the same way as other fines are enforced (see 4.11).

Charge

If there is sufficient evidence of guilt, and none of the options above is appropriate and available, the police will formally charge the suspect.

4.2   Prosecution

When an accused person is charged, the law requires that they are brought before a magistrates' court as soon as possible. There are three main methods of ensuring the defendant attends court. The first is that they have been held in custody by the police to

---

13 In police custody: police powers and suspects' rights under the revised PACE codes of practice. Home Office Research Study No. 174.
The right to silence: the impact of the Criminal Justice and Public Order Act 1994, Home Office Research Study No. 199.

appear as soon as practicable. Secondly, they may have been released on bail to attend court. Finally, a person may be summoned to appear in court. Generally, an arrest warrant may only be issued where (a) the offence is triable only on indictment (see section 3.4), or is punishable with imprisonment or (b) the address of the accused is not sufficiently established for a summons to be served.

No branch of the government or the judiciary can direct a police officer or the Crown Prosecution Service to bring criminal proceedings (or not to do so) in a particular case – this includes Ministers of the Crown. The Crown Prosecutor reviews, in accordance with criteria set out in the Code for Crown Prosecutors, all charges brought by the police (except for specified minor offences).

If the Crown Prosecution Service considers there is insufficient evidence for a realistic prospect of conviction or that prosecution is not in the public interest, it may discontinue the proceedings at any time before the start of the trial or committal.[14] Alternatively, it may consider that the evidence supports a different charge. The Crown Prosecution Service discontinued about 165,000 cases in 1999.

In most situations, any person or group of people may bring a private prosecution and commence criminal proceedings. These often occur when the Crown Prosecution Service has decided not to prosecute. If the prosecution fails, those bringing the case may be ordered to pay costs by the court, and even if the case succeeds, the costs of bringing the prosecution are not met by public funds. In certain circumstances, the CPS can take over a private prosecution either to continue or discontinue the proceedings.

As well as the CPS, other bodies also bring prosecutions. The main organisations who do this are:

- Customs and Excise
- The TV Licensing Records Office
- The Inland Revenue
- The Serious Fraud Office
- The Department of Trade and Industry
- The Driver and Vehicle Licensing Authority (DVLA)
- The Department of Social Services
- The Health and Safety Executive
- Local Authorities

14. Prosecution of Offences Act 1985 s.23.

- The National Society for the Prevention of Cruelty to Children
- The Royal Society for the Prevention of Cruelty to Animals

In magistrates' courts, 75 per cent of prosecutions are brought by the CPS. In the Crown Court the figure is about 95 per cent.

4.3 Legal representation

There are two kinds of lawyer in England and Wales, barristers and solicitors, who have distinct roles to play in the criminal justice process. Solicitors advise clients on a number of different issues and prepare cases before they get to court. They may also represent clients in court. Barristers spend a large proportion of their time representing clients in the higher courts. Recent changes have led to solicitors having wider rights of audience in these higher courts.[15]

For the Prosecution

The prosecution of a case is usually conducted by the CPS (other agencies can and do bring prosecutions – see section 4.2). At magistrates' courts this may be done by a Crown Prosecutor (a lawyer employed by the CPS), or by a solicitor or barrister from a private practice contracted by the CPS for the case. At the Crown Court, cases are presented by barristers instructed by the CPS, or by Higher Court Advocates (CPS or private practice solicitors) for cases involving guilty pleas.[16]

For the Defence

Defendants in a case are entitled to be represented by a lawyer. Representation is more common in the more serious, 'indictable' offences than in the less serious 'summary' cases.[17] The bulk of work in the magistrates' court is done by solicitors.

Legal Aid

Criminal legal aid is provided by the government which pays for the services of the lawyer selected by the accused person in cases where they cannot afford to pay for themselves. It is for courts to decide whether legal aid should be granted. Currently, this decision is based on an assessment of the person's ability to pay for their defence and on whether the provision of help is in the interests of justice. These arrangements are being streamlined under the Access to Justice Act 1999, so that in future, courts will make decisions based only on whether it is in the interests of justice. Rather than conduct a means test at the beginning of proceedings, a judge will be able to order a defendant to pay some or all of the defence costs at the end of the case.

15. As a result of the Courts and Legal Services Act 1990.
16. Changed as a result of the Access to Justice Act 1999 ss.36 and 37.
17. For definitions of indictable and summary cases see section 4.3.

The Criminal Defence Service

A new Criminal Defence Service (CDS) will be introduced in 2001. The CDS will focus on securing better quality and value for money by developing more efficient ways of providing defence services. It is intended that it will consist of a mix of private practitioners and salaried defenders. A Legal Services Commission was set up in April 2000 to oversee both the CDS and the Community Legal Service, which administers civil legal aid.

4.4   Remands

When adjourning a hearing, or committing a defendant to the Crown Court for trial or sentence, a magistrates' court may remand the defendant either in custody or on bail.

There is a statutory right to bail, but this may be denied in specific circumstances: namely where the court has substantial grounds for believing that if a defendant were remanded on bail, he or she would fail to surrender to custody; commit an offence while on bail; interfere with witnesses; or otherwise obstruct the course of justice.[18] The prosecution may, in certain circumstances, appeal to a Crown Court Judge against the decision by a magistrates' court to grant bail.[19] The appeal must be made within 48 hours. Bail may also be denied for the protection of the defendant. Where the defendant appears before the court accused or convicted of an offence allegedly committed on bail, the court need not grant bail. If a person who is summoned or released on bail fails to appear without good reason, they are said to have absconded and the court may issue a warrant for arrest. In addition to the general grounds for refusing bail, special conditions apply for young people under the age of 17 remanded in custody. See Chapter 5 for details.

Those charged with, or convicted of, homicide or rape where the defendant has a previous conviction for any of those offences should only be granted bail if there are exceptional circumstances which justify it.[20] A magistrates' court has the power to remand a defendant in custody for up to eight days in the first instance but thereafter may remand him/her for up to 28 days, provided that the defendant is present in court and has previously been remanded in custody for the same offence.[21]

---

18. Bail Act 1976.
19. Bail (Amendment) Act 1993.
20. Criminal Justice and Public Order Act 1994.
21. Magistrates' Courts Act 1980 s.128A.

Reducing delays

Early First Hearings and Early Administrative Hearings were introduced nationally in November 1999, under section 46 of the Crime and Disorder Act 1998. To reduce delays in the criminal justice process, the first hearing for bailed defendants is now typically held within one or two days of charge. Designated caseworkers, members of CPS staff who are not lawyers, have been introduced to review and present straightforward cases.

4.5   Categories of offences

Criminal offences are split into three categories as follows.

i)   Triable only on indictment

These offences are the most serious breaches of the criminal law and must be tried at the Crown Court. These 'indictable-only' offences include murder, manslaughter, rape and robbery.

ii)   Triable-either-way

These offences may be tried either at the Crown Court or at a magistrates' court. These offences include criminal damage where the value is £5,000 or greater, theft, burglary and drink driving.

iii)   Summary

These offences are triable only by a magistrates' court. This group is dominated by motoring offences for some of which fixed penalties can be issued, but also includes such offences as common assault and criminal damage up to £5,000.

4.6   Proceedings at magistrates' Courts

In 1998 1,951,900 defendants were prosecuted in magistrates' courts (including the youth court): 510,500 for indictable offences (including triable-either-way), 591,800 for summary non-motoring offences and 849,600 for summary motoring offences.

Indictable-only offences

Currently, in the case of indictable-only offences, magistrates must consider (in *committal* proceedings) whether there is a case to answer. If the magistrates decide that there is, the case will be committed to the Crown Court. Since the 1996 Criminal Procedure and Investigations Act, this process has been simplified, and is known as a committal 'on the papers'. Only documentary evidence is now considered. Witnesses are not called or cross-examined.

In serious or complex fraud cases, and those involving child witnesses, there is provision for the prosecutor to lodge a notice with the magistrates' court, stating that the case should be immediately *transferred* to the Crown Court. These cases then automatically transfer, and a judge is assigned to the case and hears any application to dismiss the charges.

Measures to speed up the justice process for defendants charged with indictable-only offences are being piloted and evaluated.[22] These measures mean that an offender charged with indictable-only offences is sent immediately to the Crown Court. Magistrates may consider bail and other minor issues, but they do not consider whether there is a case to answer.

Triable-either-way offences

For a triable-either-way offence, magistrates have to decide whether to try the case themselves or to commit the case for trial to the Crown Court. Twelve per cent of those adults proceeded against for triable-either-way cases were committed to the Crown Court for trial in 1998, and a further four per cent of defendants in triable-either-way cases were committed for sentence.

Since October 1997, magistrates have been able to hear the defendant's plea before making a decision on where the case should be tried. This procedure is known as 'Plea Before Venue'.[23] Under the new system, if the defendant indicates a guilty plea, the magistrates are required to convict the offender, and either pass sentence or commit the defendant to the Crown Court for sentence if the magistrates feel that the appropriate sentence is beyond their powers (magistrates can sentence up to six months in prison and fine up to £5,000). If the defendant indicates a not guilty plea, the magistrates must decide whether they consider the case is too serious to be dealt with summarily. Hence, under this new procedure, some defendants who would have been committed for trial to the Crown Court under the old system will be dealt with entirely by proceedings in magistrates' courts or be committed for sentence to the Crown Court thereby reducing the numbers committed for trial. A comparison of 1998 figures with those for 1997 shows that the number of defendants committed for sentence increased by 11,900 and the number committed for trial decreased by 14,300. These changes are likely to reflect the influence of plea before venue proceedings.

When the charge is for several offences, some of which are triable-either-way and others summarily, and the triable-either-way offences are transferred for trial, certain specific summary offences may also be included on the indictment, including driving while

---

22. Under The Crime and Disorder Act 1998.
23. Crime (Sentences) Act 1997.

disqualified, common assault and taking a motor vehicle without authority. However, the Crown Court may only pass sentences that are within magistrates' powers for these offences.

Even if the magistrates decide not to commit the case to Crown Court, the defendant may elect to be tried by jury. In 1998, 28 per cent of committals to the Crown Court for trial for triable-either-way offences were as a result of defendant election.

Mode of trial

The government is proposing to abolish a defendant's ability to elect for jury trial in triable-either-way cases. Magistrates alone would then have the power to decide where the case is tried. The aim is to reduce the costs and delays that occur when a case is committed to the Crown Court. In many of the cases where the defendant elects Crown Court trial, they plead guilty before the case is tried. A right to appeal to the Crown Court would be introduced where the defendant wanted to press for jury trial.

4.7   Proceedings before magistrates

On summary trial the court will read the charge to the accused and ask whether they plead guilty or not guilty. If the accused pleads not guilty, the court will hear evidence and may convict the accused or dismiss the case. Over 90 per cent of defendants on summary trial plead guilty. In this case, the court will usually hear an outline of the case from the prosecution and then proceed to the sentencing stage. However, where the defendant pleads guilty and then says something which indicates a defence to the charge or says, for example, that the plea is entered 'to get the case over with', the guilty plea must be rejected. If the prosecutor appears but the accused fails to appear as requested then the court, on proof of service of summons, may proceed in their absence or adjourn the hearing or, in certain cases, issue a warrant for arrest. If the accused appears but the prosecutor does not, the court may dismiss the case or adjourn the trial. Where the offender is convicted, the court may proceed to sentence immediately or may adjourn if further information is required before sentencing. Defendants may be invited to plead guilty for certain summary (mostly motoring) offences by post and therefore avoid a court appearance.

4.8 Trial at Crown Court

Just over four per cent of those proceeded against are dealt with by the Crown Court. Of these, around 60 per cent plead guilty.[24] As at the magistrates' court, in these cases the judge will move to the sentencing stage of the process. A jury is not involved in these cases.

Crown Court trial for defendants pleading not guilty is before a judge and jury. A jury consists of 12 persons randomly selected from a list of all those persons aged 18 to 70 who registered as electors and are neither ineligible nor disqualified. These jurors take an oath:

"I swear by Almighty God that I will faithfully try the defendant and give a true verdict according to the evidence."

The duty of the jury is to listen to the evidence and to give their verdict as to whether the accused is guilty or not guilty. The accused and the prosecution have the right to challenge any juror if it is believed they are known to someone involved in the case or if they appear unable to understand the proceedings. The verdict of the jury in criminal proceedings need not be unanimous but must be at least ten to two. If the verdict is guilty, the judge of the court pronounces sentence. The court may order a convicted offender to pay the whole or any part of the costs incurred by the prosecution. On acquittal, the court may order the payment of defence costs from the central funds.

4.9   Disclosure of evidence

The Criminal Procedure and Investigations Act 1996 created a statutory scheme for prosecution and defence disclosure of evidence in criminal proceedings. The prosecution is required to disclose to the accused any material they have knowledge of which, in the prosecutor's opinion, might undermine the prosecution case. If there is no such evidence, a written statement to this effect must be given to the accused. The defendant is required,

---

24. 62 per cent in 1998. Due to plea before venue procedures (section 3.4), this figure has dropped from 67 per
    cent in 1997. Criminal Statistics 1998.

under certain conditions, to give a statement setting out the general nature of the defence. If this is done, the prosecution is then required to make a second disclosure of any information that might assist the defence. The defence also has the right to apply for a court order requiring the disclosure of prosecution evidence if the accused has reasonable cause to believe there exists prosecution material that may aid their defence.

4.10   Sentencing

Under a statutory framework for sentencing introduced in the Criminal Justice Act 1991 (and amended by the Criminal Justice Act 1993), courts are generally required to impose sentences which reflect the seriousness of the offence or offences committed by the offender. The Act does not define 'seriousness'. The Court of Appeal has provided guidance on interpretation since the Act came into effect in October 1992. In deciding what sentence to impose, the judge or magistrate will take account of:

i)   The facts of the offence, which have been presented in court, including any aggravating or mitigating factors. In addition, a defendant pleading guilty may wish to admit other similar offences and such offences may be taken into consideration for the purpose of sentence without the offender being formally convicted of them and with no separate penalty being imposed.

ii) The circumstances of the offender. In the Crown Court, the prosecution will provide a statement known as 'the antecedents' covering details of the offence, previous convictions and sentences. In addition, a pre-sentence report (PSR) giving fuller information may be prepared for the court by a probation officer. This report contains information about the character, personality and social and domestic background of the defendant; educational record and information about employment (if any), assessment of impact on victim and risk of reoffending. It will include a proposal as to what community sentence (e.g. probation order) would be most suitable for the offender if the court was to decide that such a sentence would be appropriate. In some cases, a specific sentence report (SSR) will be prepared by the Probation Service. This is similar to a PSR, but focuses only on the suitability of a particular sentence. SSRs speed up the process when it is likely that a particular sentence – most often community service or a probation order – will be given.

Plea in mitigation

If a defence lawyer is present, they will make a speech in mitigation on behalf of the offender to give the court the defendant's explanation of the offence and any other matters going in the defendant's favour. This might include information about an early guilty plea.

Pleading guilty at an early stage in the proceedings usually leads to a shorter sentence – this is known as a sentence discount. Judges and magistrates are required, when sentencing an offender who has pleaded guilty, to take into account the stage at which the guilty plea was entered, and the circumstances in which the plea was made.[25] If a discounted sentence is passed, this must be stated in court. The Court of Appeal states that a discount of one-third should normally be given for a timely guilty plea.

4.11   Principal sentences for adults

Imprisonment

Imprisonment is the most severe penalty available to the courts, and is only available for more serious offences. Courts have the power to impose a sentence up to a maximum term specified by the Act of Parliament which created the particular offence. Under the Criminal Justice Act 1991, a custodial sentence can normally only be imposed if the offence is 'so serious' that only such a penalty can be justified for the offence or to protect the public from serious harm from a violent or sexual offender. The maximum custodial penalty reflects the gravity of the worst possible case and is thus high for the most serious offences, e.g. life imprisonment for murder (for which it is mandatory), rape, robbery or manslaughter and 14 years for domestic burglary. A magistrates' court may not sentence to more than six months (or less than five days) for any one offence and no longer than 12 months in total, where sentences are being imposed for two or more triable-either-way offences and are to run consecutively. Where an offender is sentenced to imprisonment for several offences, the sentences may be ordered by the court to run either consecutively or concurrently, depending on a number of factors. Consecutive sentences will generally be appropriate, for example, where different types of offending behaviour are concerned.

The Crime (Sentences) Act 1997 requires courts to impose minimum sentences on offenders committing repeat, serious offences. These include a mandatory sentence of life imprisonment for anyone over the age of 18 convicted of a serious offence who has a previous conviction for a similar offence. These serious offences include murder, attempted murder, manslaughter, rape, violent offences (such as grievous bodily harm), and armed robbery. This sentence is automatic unless the court finds exceptional circumstances. There is also provision for a minimum prison sentence of seven years for a person over the age of 18, convicted of a class A drug trafficking offence who has two or more previous convictions for similar offences; and a minimum of three years imprisonment for a third offence of domestic burglary. These sentences should be imposed unless the court finds that they would be unjust in all the circumstances.

---

25. Criminal Justice and Public Order Act 1994.

Life imprisonment

Life imprisonment, or its equivalent, must be imposed on all persons aged ten and over convicted of murder. It is also available for a number of the most serious crimes, including manslaughter, robbery, rape, assault with intent to do grievous bodily harm, aggravated burglary and certain firearms offences. For these offences, the court may choose instead to impose a prison sentence of a specified length or a non-custodial penalty. Additionally, there is a requirement for a life sentence for those convicted of a second serious offence (see above).

There is no entitlement to release during a life sentence but offenders may be considered for release on licence. All life sentence prisoners are initially released under the supervision of a probation officer. The reporting conditions of the licence may be lifted after a period of time if the individual has demonstrated that such restrictions are unnecessary.

For those serving a mandatory life sentence (i.e. for murder), release may only be authorised by the Home Secretary on the recommendation of the Parole Board and after consulting the Lord Chief Justice and, if available, the trial judge. There are special arrangements for those aged under 21 who are found guilty of murder – see Chapter 5.

For discretionary lifers (offenders who receive life sentences as a maximum, rather than a mandatory sentence or who are sentenced to life for repeat offences), the sentencing court is able to specify a term after which the prisoner should be eligible for release procedures. When this term has been served the discretionary life sentence prisoner is entitled to require the Home Secretary to refer the case to the Parole Board. The Board has the power to direct the Home Secretary to release the prisoner on licence if satisfied that custody is no longer necessary for the protection of the public. For discretionary life prisoners, the Home Secretary has no power to reject a recommendation by the Parole Board. These arrangements apply to prisoners of all ages, including young offenders.

Suspended sentence

Where the court decides that the offence is sufficiently serious to justify a sentence of not more than two years' imprisonment, the sentence may be suspended for between one and two years if there are exceptional circumstances for doing so. In the rare cases where a suspended sentence is passed, the court should consider adding a fine or compensation order. The suspended prison sentence is not served at all, unless the offender commits a further imprisonable offence during its operational period.

Community sentences

The Criminal Justice Act 1991 increased and strengthened the range of punishments which are available in the community. They are now regarded as penalties in their own right and not as alternatives to custody. A community sentence can only be imposed when the offence is 'serious enough' to warrant that penalty. The restrictions on liberty imposed by a particular order must be commensurate with the seriousness of the offence and be the most suitable for the offender. Imposition of a community penalty was dependent on the consent of the offender until October 1997, when this condition was repealed by the Crime (Sentences) Act 1997. If an offender fails to attend, or breaks the order, this is known as a 'breach'. There are national standards for dealing with breaches and these can lead to the offender being given a custodial term. Some community penalties are likely to be renamed towards the end of 2000.[26] Community service orders will be renamed 'community punishment orders', Probation orders will be known as 'community rehabilitation orders' and Combination orders will become 'community punishment and rehabilitation orders'. The community penalties available are:

(i) Community service orders

An offender aged 16 or over who is convicted of an offence for which a court can send an adult to prison may be required to perform unpaid work on behalf of the community. Such orders involve a minimum of 40 hours and a maximum of 240 hours to be completed within 12 months. The work is under the direction of a community service organiser, working within the Probation Service. A wide variety of work is done including, for example, outdoor conservation projects, building adventure playgrounds, and painting and decorating for the elderly or disabled.

(ii) Probation orders

An offender aged 16 or over may be sentenced to a probation order for a period ranging from six months to three years. A court may make a probation order in the interests of securing the rehabilitation of the offender; protecting the public from harm; or preventing the commission of further offences. Probation orders require the offender to be supervised by a probation officer. Additionally the court has the power to include any other requirement considered appropriate. This could include residence at a specified address, activities, attendance at a probation centre, treatment for a mental condition and treatment for drug or alcohol dependency. Some probation centres run courses which offenders may attend for up to 60 days as a requirement of a probation order.

26. Under the Criminal Justice and Court Services Bill.

(iii) Combination orders

This order was introduced in October 1992 by the Criminal Justice Act 1991. It combines elements of both probation supervision and community service and may be given to any offender aged 16 or over. The maximum duration of the probation element of the combination order is three years and the minimum 12 months. When a combination order is made, probation supervision continues for at least as long as community service is being performed. The minimum number of community service hours is 40 and the maximum 100.

(iv) Curfew orders

Curfew orders require an offender to remain, for specific periods, at a specific address.[27] Electronically monitored curfew orders have been available nationally since December 1999.[28] This involves the offender wearing an electronic 'tag' which, in combination with equipment located at the curfew address, monitors when the offender is at the address. If the offender leaves the address during curfew hours, or attempts to move or damage the equipment or tag, the private sector companies which monitor the schemes are alerted. Curfew orders can be made in addition to another community penalty.

(v) Drug treatment and testing orders

Drug treatment and testing orders are aimed at those who commit crimes to fund a drug habit. These orders are due to be available nationally from the end of 2000. The offender is required to undergo treatment for their drug problem. The order can be made either on its own, or with another community order. An offender must be aged 16 or over, considered to be a suitable candidate, and must consent to the order. The order requires the offender to undergo a treatment programme and to submit to regular testing. The order can last between six months and three years.

Fines

A court may fine an offender for any offence (except murder or treason), although a court will not normally impose a fine for more serious offences except in conjunction with another penalty. The 1993 Criminal Justice Act requires all courts to set fines which reflect the seriousness of the offence and which also take into account the financial circumstances of the offender. Magistrates can only impose fines up to £5,000.

Courts can allow offenders to pay the fine in regular instalments, usually over the course of 12 months. The task of ensuring that payments are made is carried out by magistrates' courts. Where appropriate, the court can have payments deducted from an offender's wage or benefits, or issue a distress warrant to seize a defaulter's property. If all other available methods have been tried or considered in an attempt to elicit payment, the final sanction is imprisonment,

27. Criminal Justice Act 1991.
28. Criminal Justice Act 1991 s.12.

with the sentence length dependent upon the amount outstanding. In 1999, there were 3,727 receptions to prison for fine default. This accounted for three per cent of all receptions. Because fine defaulters are generally sentenced to short terms, the percentage of the sentenced prison population who are fine defaulters at any one time is small (about 0.2% of the prison population on 30th June 1999). The number of defaulters sent to prison decreased substantially from 1988, after a Queens' Bench judgement clarified the present legislative position whereby all available options must be considered before imprisoning a defaulter.[29]

Discharge

A court may discharge a convicted person either absolutely or conditionally, where the court takes the view that it is not necessary to impose punishment. An absolute discharge requires nothing from the offender and imposes no restrictions on future conduct. The majority of discharges are, however, conditional discharges, where the offender remains liable to punishment for the offence if convicted of a further offence within whatever period (not more than three years) that the court may specify.

Compensation

In cases involving death, injury, loss or damage, the courts are required to consider making a compensation order, and to give reasons where no such order is made. A compensation order can also be made in addition to any other sentence or order, or can be the only sentence imposed for a particular offence. A magistrates' court can order compensation up to a maximum of £5,000 per offence, but there is no such limit in the Crown Court. However, courts are required to have regard to the means of the offender when deciding whether to make a compensation order and when deciding on its amount. When the defendant makes payments against financial penalties, compensation orders are paid off before fines.

Capital punishment

Capital punishment for murder was abolished in 1965, but was retained, although unused, for treason and some other miscellaneous offences. It was abolished for these remaining offences under section 36 of the Crime and Disorder Act in September 1998.

Other sentences

A range of other sentences are available to the courts, including confiscation orders, exclusion orders and disqualification from driving. Although not a sentence, a convicted person may be the subject of a bind-over (as may any witness or party appearing before the court). A bind-over requires the individual to keep the peace for a fixed period of time, specified by the court.

---

29. R v Oldham Justices, ex parte Cawley [1995] QBD.

4.12   Appeals

In criminal matters, the Crown Court deals mainly with appeals by persons convicted in magistrates' courts against their conviction or sentence or both. Appeals may be limited to conviction only or to part of a sentence (e.g. a compensation order or driving disqualification) and the Crown Court may, if it considers it appropriate, vary all or part of a sentence. The Criminal Division of the Court of Appeal hears appeals in criminal matters from the Crown Court. Courts are constituted by the Lord Chief Justice and Lords Justices assisted by High Court Judges as required. A further appeal may be made to the House of Lords where it has been certified by the Court of Appeal Criminal Division that a point of law of general public importance was involved in the decision. The Attorney General has the power to refer unduly lenient sentences for offences triable on indictment to the Court of Appeal. This power was extended in January 1994 to certain triable-either-way cases.

The Criminal Cases Review Commission was set up as a result of The Criminal Appeal Act 1995, which followed an investigation by the Royal Commission on Criminal Justice into the effectiveness of the CJS. The Commission is an independent body responsible for investigating suspected miscarriages of criminal justice. If a case has already been through the appeals system and has not succeeded for any reason, the individual may apply to the

Commission. The Commission may then investigate the case and will decide whether or not to refer the case to the appropriate appeal court.

4.13   Early release from custody

All prison inmates are eligible for release before the end of their sentence. The current schemes stem from the recommendations of the Carlisle Review Committee and were introduced from 1 October 1992 by the Criminal Justice Act 1991. The arrangements for the early release of determinate sentence prisoners also apply to young offenders, including those detained under Section 53(2) of the Children and Young Persons Act 1933.

Prisoners may have additional days awarded as a disciplinary sanction. These will delay all release and supervision expiry dates. Additional days will not extend the original sentence; i.e. they can only go up to the 100 per cent point.

All prisoners are eligible for release at the half-way point of sentence (subject to additional days). All those released are considered to be 'at risk' until the end of the sentence – if they are convicted of further imprisonable offences committed before the period of sentence has fully expired, the court may reactivate all or part of the original sentence outstanding at the time the new offence was committed, in addition to any new sentence it may impose.

For those prisoners sentenced from 1 October 1992, the following are the variations in early release arrangements based upon sentence length.

The Automatic Unconditional Release Scheme (AUR)

All inmates sentenced to under 12 months are released automatically half-way through their sentence. There is no compulsory supervision except for young offenders who are subject to statutory supervision for a minimum of three months, or until the offender's 22nd birthday if that is sooner.

The Automatic Conditional Release Scheme (ACR)

All inmates sentenced to between 12 months and four years are released automatically half way through their sentence on a licence (issued on behalf of the Home Secretary by the Governor). Offenders are subject to compulsory supervision up to the three-quarters point of sentence. Some sex offenders may be supervised up to the 100 per cent point of their sentence at the direction of the sentencing judge. Individuals who breach their licence conditions are subject to executive recall to prison.[30] Prior to 1999 these individuals were dealt with by magistrates' courts.

---

30. Crime and Disorder Act 1998 s.103.

The Discretionary Conditional Release Scheme (DCR)

All inmates sentenced to four years and over become eligible for release on parole at the half-way point of sentence. All cases are considered by the Parole Board at regular intervals (usually annually) until the two-thirds point of sentence. Those not selected for parole within this period are released automatically on licence at the two-thirds point.

For inmates sentenced to less than 15 years, the Home Secretary has delegated the decision on release to the Parole Board. For prisoners sentenced to 15 years and over, the Parole Board makes a recommendation but the final decision rests with the Home Secretary.

All inmates are supervised until the three-quarters point of sentence. Some sex offenders are supervised to the 100 per cent point at the discretion of the sentencing judge. Recall to prison for breach of licence conditions is dealt with by the Parole Board.

Home Detention Curfew (HDC)

The scheme was introduced from 28 January 1999 by the Crime and Disorder Act 1998.

Prisoners sentenced to custody for three months or more, but less than four years, are, in principle, eligible to be released on HDC. Prisoners must be aged 18 or over at the release date. Prisoners can be released up to two months early, but are required to be at a specific address for at least nine hours a day, monitored by an electronic tag. There are some exclusions, including most prisoners required to register under Part 1 of the Sex Offenders Act 1997, those convicted of breaching a curfew order and those facing deportation. All eligible prisoners must pass a risk assessment and have a suitable address before they will be granted HDC. The final decision is made by the prison governor.

The HDC runs alongside other supervision demanded by the early release procedure appropriate to the sentence length. Any prisoner released on HDC can be recalled if they break the terms of their curfew, or present a danger to the public. They will also be recalled if there is a change of circumstances (e.g. they lose their accommodation), it is impossible to monitor them (e.g. if there is no suitable and constant electricity supply), or they are charged with a new offence.

4.14   What works?

Since 1980, there has been an increasing focus on establishing 'what works' in sentencing, particularly in relation to community sentences. Rehabilitation has traditionally been seen as an aim more closely associated with probation and community sentences rather than with the prison system. Optimism about the ability of community sentences to rehabilitate has been growing, and the Probation Service now attempts to establish 'what works' in terms of reducing reoffending for different community sentences. This has traditionally been measured using reconviction rates. However, there are some drawbacks to using these. For instance, they do not measure offence severity, and only cover those incidents of reoffending where the individual is caught. Therefore these reconviction rates are often combined with measures of attitude and behavioural change in order to fully evaluate the effectiveness of community penalties.

5. Youth justice

5.1 Youth Justice Board

The Youth Justice Board (YJB) for England and Wales, which became operational on 30 September 1998, maintains oversight of the operation of the YOTs and the youth justice system as a whole. It is a non-departmental public body, sponsored by the Home Office. The Board consists of between ten and 12 members appointed by the Secretary of State, including people who have extensive recent experience of the youth justice system. The functions of the Board include:

- monitoring the operation of the youth justice system and the provision of youth justice services
- advising the Secretary of State on this and on the setting of national standards for the provision of youth justice services and custodial accommodation
- advising on how the principal aim of the youth justice system might most effectively be pursued
- identifying and promoting, and making grants for the development of, good practice, including good practice in the operation of the youth justice system and the prevention of youth offending
- since April 2000, the YJB has been responsible for commissioning places for children and young people remanded and sentenced by the courts to secure facilities.

The Crime and Disorder Act 1998 placed a statutory duty on the Youth Justice Board and all those working in the youth justice system to have regard to the principal aim of preventing offending by children and young people. This is to be achieved through six key objectives:

- swift administration of justice
- ensuring young people face up to the consequences of their offending
- ensuring the risk factors associated with offending are addressed in any intervention
- punishment proportionate to the seriousness and frequency of offending
- encouraging reparation by young offenders to their victims
- reinforcing parental responsibility.

5.2   Youth Offending Teams (YOTs)

The Crime and Disorder Act 1998 introduced new structures at local and national level to provide the framework to tackle youth offending. From 1 April 2000 Youth Offending Teams (YOTs) have brought together the staff and wider resources of the police, social services, the Probation Service, education and health, in the delivery of youth justice services, with the scope to involve others, including the voluntary sector.

5.3   Reprimands and final warnings

A new reprimand and final warning scheme has replaced police cautioning of young offenders. Reprimands can be given to first-time offenders for minor offences. Any further offending results in either a final warning or a charge. The final warning triggers immediate referral to a local YOT which will assess the young person and, unless they consider it inappropriate, prepare a rehabilitation programme (or 'change' programme, as it is now known) designed to tackle the reasons for the young person's offending behaviour and to prevent any future offending. This assessment will usually involve contacting the victim to assess whether victim/offender mediation (see restorative justice textbox in 5.6) or some form of reparation to the victim or community is appropriate

5.4   Youth Courts

Young people aged between 10 and 17 inclusive are mainly dealt with in the youth courts by specially trained magistrates. The youth court was introduced from 1st October 1992 and replaced the juvenile court, established in 1908, which dealt with offenders only up to and including those aged 16.[31] In youth courts, no person is allowed to be present unless authorised by the court, except for the members and officers of the court, parties to the case (normally including parents/guardians), their legal representatives, witnesses and bona fide representatives of the media. Proceedings may be reported in the press but the young person may not generally be identified.

A child or young person is generally tried in the youth court unless any of the below apply:

a) he or she is charged with homicide (e.g. murder or manslaughter), when they must be sent to the Crown Court for trial

b) he or she is aged 14 or over and is charged with a 'grave crime' (an offence for which an adult could be imprisoned for at least 14 years), indecent assault or dangerous driving. These cases may be sent to the Crown Court if magistrates decide that if convicted, the appropriate sentence would be more than they have the power to give

---

31. Criminal Justice Act 1991 s.70.

c) he or she is charged jointly with another person aged 18 or more, when both should be dealt with in the Crown Court.

Statutory time limits (STLs)

STLs will allow time limits to be set for each stage of criminal proceedings involving young offenders, with the exception of the trial itself. The aim of these time limits is to speed up the processes of dealing with young offenders. The time limit for the period between the first appearance in the youth court and the start of the trial was provided for (but not implemented) by the Prosecution of Offences Act 1985 and is set at 99 days. The Crime and Disorder Act 1998 allows for the introduction of STLs for young offenders for the periods between arrest and the date set for first appearance in court (36 days), and between conviction to sentence (29 days). Extensions to these limits may be requested by the police or prosecution if there is good reason. If the time limits are exceeded without an extension being granted then the case must be discontinued. In order to reinstate the case fresh proceedings will have to be started.

Time limit pilots started on 1 November 1999, with a view to national implementation in 2002, subject to the results of the 18-month pilots.

Remands - Young people under 17 who are charged and not released on bail will usually be remanded to local authority accommodation. Conditions such as a curfew can be imposed on the child and the authority.

Secure Remands – Since June 1999, courts have had the power under the Crime and Disorder Act 1998 to order a secure remand direct to local authority accommodation. This is available for females aged 12 to 16 and males aged 12 to 14 where the child is charged with or convicted of a violent or sexual offence, or an offence where an adult could be sentenced to 14 years or more imprisonment. It is also available for the same age groups if there is a recent history of absconding while remanded to local authority accommodation and if the young person is charged or convicted of an imprisonable offence committed while remanded. Additionally, the court must be of the opinion that only a remand to secure accommodation would be adequate to protect the public. In the case of boys aged 15 and 16, secure remands (ordered under the same conditions as above) will generally be to prison service accommodation. In exceptional cases where the boy is deemed vulnerable, the remand may be made to secure local authority accommodation.[32]

---

32. Secure remands are allowed for under s.23 of the Children and Young Persons Act 1969, but amended under the Crime and Disorder Act 1998.

5.5   Custodial Sentences

Detention and Training Orders

Detention and Training Orders were introduced by the Crime and Disorder Act 1998 and came into effect on 1 April 2000. It is the new main custodial sentence for juveniles and replaces the secure training order for 12- to 14- year-olds and detention in a young offender institution for 15- to 17- year-olds. It is a two part sentence which combines a period in custody with a period spent under supervision in the community. Subject to provisions for early or late release, half the term of the order is spent in custody and half under supervision in the community. The emphasis is on clear sentence planning to ensure that time spent in custody is spent constructively and followed up by effective supervision and support on release.

Detention and training orders are available for 12- to 17- year-olds for any imprisonable offence sufficiently serious to justify custody under section 1 of the Criminal Justice Act 1991. If the child or young person is aged 12 to 14 the court must be of the opinion that he or she is a persistent offender. The Crime and Disorder Act also provides for detention and training orders to be available for 10- to 11- year-old persistent offenders, but this power is not currently in use.

The Detention and Training order is available to the youth court and the Crown Court. The court can impose an order of between four and 24 months provided it does not exceed the maximum term that could be imposed on an adult offender by the Crown Court.

Custody arrangements for serious offences

Anyone found guilty of murder committed when under the age of 18 must be sentenced to 'detention during Her Majesty's pleasure'(see textbox overleaf).[33] A person aged under 18 convicted of an offence other than murder for which a life sentence may be passed on an adult may be sentenced to 'detention for life'.[34] Currently, a person convicted of murder who is aged 18 or over at the time of the offence but under 21 on conviction must be sentenced to 'custody for life'. This is also the maximum penalty when an offender aged 18 to 20 is convicted of any other offence for which an adult offender would be liable to life imprisonment. However, the Criminal Justice and Court Services Bill, expected to be made law in late 2000, will change the law so that all convicted defendants aged 18 or over at the time of conviction will be sentenced as adults. Release procedures for juveniles are the same as those for adults as described in Chapter 4.

---

33. Children and Young Persons Act 1933 s.53.
34. Criminal Justice Act 1988 s.8.

Tariff setting for those under 18

Historically, the Home Secretary has had the power to set the tariff to be served in cases where an individual has been sentenced to be detained during Her Majesty's Pleasure as a result of committing murder under the age of 18. However, in December 1999, the European Court of Human Rights in the case of Thompson and Venables (the boys who killed James Bulger in 1993) found that this was in breach of the European Convention of Human Rights. The Criminal Justice and Court Services Bill, which is due to be passed by Parliament in late 2000, will give the sentencing court the task of setting the tariff to be served.

5.6   Non-custodial sentences

Where the youth court sees fit, all young offenders may be given absolute and conditional discharges as for adults (see 4.11). Young offenders aged 16 and over may receive a probation order, a community service order, or a combination order in the same way as adults (see Chapter 4). Young offenders aged 10 to 17 may also be fined, but in certain cases their parent or guardian can be ordered to pay.

Supervision Order

This may be given to any young offender and can last between three months and three years. It requires that the young person is supervised by either a probation officer, the local authority or a member of the YOT. They are required to meet with their supervisor at regular intervals and may also be required to undertake what are known as 'specified activities' to help them address their offending behaviour. The Crime and Disorder Act allows an element of reparation to be attached to the order. This works in the same way as the Reparation Order described below.

Attendance Centre Order

The aim of this order is that the offender should be 'given, under supervision, appropriate occupation and instruction'. This order may be given to any offender aged between 10 and 20. For those 18 or over the maximum period of the order is 36 hours, but in the case of those aged under 18 the order must be for 12 hours unless there are exceptional circumstances when it may be reduced or increased. The order requires the young person to attend a local centre for a maximum of three hours per day where they usually receive instruction on social skills and physical training.

Restorative Justice

The Crime and Disorder Act 1998 introduced three new orders for young offenders – the final warning (p.48), the reparation order and the action plan order (see below) – which incorporate Restorative Justice principles in that they all allow for the involvement of the victim in determining the appropriate course of action. In addition schemes exist for offenders of all ages after sentence.

Restorative Justice is a participative process in which the parties directly affected by an offence are actively involved in its resolution, with help from a facilitator. It seeks to balance the concerns of the victim and the community with the need to reintegrate the offender into society. Restorative Justice may involve enabling offenders to understand the consequences of their actions, hearing the views of victims and arranging reparation.

The most common form of Restorative Justice is victim-offender mediation. The victim and offender are helped by a facilitator to reach an agreement. They may or may not meet face to face. Some forms of Restorative Justice involve the families or supporters of both the victim and the offender.

Reparation Orders

A reparation order requires an offender to make specified reparation to their victim, if that victim consents, or to the community at large. Reparation under the order might involve writing a letter of apology, apologising to the victim in person, cleaning graffiti or repairing criminal damage for which the offender has been responsible. The order aims to help young offenders understand and face up to the consequences of their actions, and offer some practical recompense to victims. The reparation must be commensurate with the seriousness of the offence for which the order is being given, but may not exceed a total of 24 hours in aggregate. YOTs are responsible for co-ordinating arrangements for the provision of reports to the courts and communicating with the victim to ascertain whether reparation is appropriate. A reparation order cannot be combined with a custodial sentence, or with a community service order, a combination order, a supervision order or an action plan order.

Action Plan Orders

The action plan order is designed to provide a short but intensive and individually tailored response to offending behaviour, so that the causes of that offending as well as the offending itself can be addressed. This may include making reparation to the victim if this is considered appropriate and the victim consents. The order places certain requirements on the young offender who is supervised by a responsible officer. These requirements must last for three months in total.

The referral order - The Youth Justice and Criminal Evidence Act 1999 introduced a new disposal for young offenders based on restorative justice principles - the referral order. Following a conviction, a first time offender who has pleaded guilty will be referred to a youth offender panel, unless the court decides that a discharge or custody is appropriate. This panel will be made up of people recruited from the local community, who have an interest or expertise in dealing with young people. The panel will also include a member of the local YOT. The panel will agree a contract with the offender and their family aimed at tackling the young person's offending behaviour and its causes. The contract will set out clear requirements that they will have to fulfil. These might include an apology and some form of reparation to their victim, carrying out community work, taking part in family counselling or drug rehabilitation. If they fail to agree or breach the terms of a contract the young person will be returned to the court for sentencing for the original offence. This order is being piloted in seven areas from Summer 2000 with a view to national implementation in 2002 subject to the outcome of an evaluation of the pilots.

Parental bind-overs

Where it is judged that parents or guardians have not exercised proper care and control over the youth, the court may order a parental bind-over. This requires parents or guardians to exercise proper care and control over the youth or to be liable for the sum specified. This may not exceed £1,000. In the case of young persons under 16, courts must give reasons for not binding over parents or guardians. Parental bind-overs are discretionary for courts in the case of 16- and 17- year-olds. The period of the bind-over may not exceed three years or until the young person reaches the age of 18.

Parenting Orders

The parenting order aims to help reinforce and support parental responsibility. Introduced in the Crime and Disorder Act 1998 it can consist of two elements: a requirement on the parent or guardian to attend counselling or guidance sessions which can last for up to three months; and requirements encouraging the parent or guardian to exercise a measure of control over the child (e.g. that the parent or guardian ensures that the child attends school or avoids certain people or places which had adversely affected the child's behaviour). These can last for up to 12 months. The requirements will be overseen by a probation officer, a social worker or a member of a youth offending team.

6   Victims and witnesses

6.1   The Victim's Charter

The Victim's Charter was first published in 1990 and subsequently revised in 1996. It sets out what sort of service victims of crime should expect. It informs victims of their rights in such areas as their right to information regarding the case, their right to explain how the offence has affected them and their right to be treated with sensitivity and to be supported if they have to attend court. The Victim's Steering Group monitors the standards of service set out in the revised edition of the Charter. The Group is chaired by the Home Office and includes representatives from all the agencies involved in providing a service to victims.

6.2   Vulnerable and intimidated witnesses

In June 1998 the report 'Speaking up for Justice' was published, addressing the need to introduce measures to support and protect vulnerable and intimidated witnesses. The report was produced by a working group including representatives from victim support and the police, as well as government departments. In July 1999, the Youth Justice and Criminal Evidence Act introduced a number of the recommendations of the report. These included:

- a ban on the cross-examination of victims of rape and sexual assault by unrepresented defendants; and greater restrictions on questioning a rape victim about their sexual history
- video-recorded evidence, live CCTV links, screens and communications aids to be introduced for adult and child witnesses likely to be intimidated and distressed by facing the defendant in court. This will be introduced in the Crown Court by the end of 2000
- pagers for intimidated witnesses so that they do not have to wait at court buildings in the same room as the defendant.

6.3   The Courts' Charter

The Courts' Charter, published by the Court Service, was developed to ensure that all users of the Crown Court know what to expect from their dealings with the courts. This includes standards of service and performance. The Charter states that fair and equal treatment will be given regardless of race, ethnic origin, disability, gender, sexual orientation or religious beliefs. Also included is information about procedures at court and avenues for complaints. There are separate versions of the charter for users of different courts, and for different types of user (e.g. defendants, witnesses, jurors and legal professionals). Similar quality of service charters are produced by each Magistrates' Courts Committee.

6.4   Victim Support

Victim Support is an independent charity which receives financial support from the government. It offers help and support to victims of crime. The police tell Victim Support about cases or will ask victims if they want to be put in touch with Victim Support.

Victim Support's services are free and confidential. Staff and volunteers come from all sections of the local community and are specially trained. Victim Support offers emotional support, practical help such as help with claims for insurance or criminal injuries compensation, and information about other organisations which may be able to help with specific problems.

6.5   The Witness Service

The Witness Service operates in all Crown Court centres in England and Wales. The service is staffed by paid co-ordinators and volunteers, who are trained in accordance with the service's code of practice. The Witness Service offers:

- someone to talk to in confidence
- a visit and look round the court before being called
- information on court procedures
- someone to accompany the witness into the court room when giving evidence
- practical help
- contact with appropriate people for different types of information.

Witness Services are now being extended to cover magistrates' courts as well as Crown Court centres.

6.6   Compensation

There are two sources of compensation for a victim of crime. If someone is found guilty of an offence, the court must consider ordering them to pay compensation (financial penalty) for any loss, injury or damage suffered by the victim. Compensation is limited to what the offender can reasonably afford, so may not cover the loss or injury in full. Financial penalties are often paid in instalments, and where there is a mix of fines and compensation the compensation to the victim takes precedence over the fine.

Compensation is available for some victims of violent crime under the Criminal Injuries Compensation Scheme (CICS). This provides government funded payment to victims of crimes of violence who are judged to be blameless and those injured in trying to apprehend criminals or prevent crime. Anyone sustaining injury in England, Scotland and Wales is eligible to apply. There are separate arrangements in Northern Ireland. Someone does not have to be found guilty of the crime in order for the victim to be able to claim compensation.[35]

The original scheme was introduced in 1964. It was non-statutory, with compensation being assessed by the Criminal Injuries Compensation Board (CICB) on the basis of common law damages (what an applicant could expect to be awarded in a successful action for damages in the civil courts). The terms of the original scheme were modified in 1969, 1979 and again in 1990. Each change extended the scheme's scope to certain classes of victim previously excluded. But the scheme was changed more fundamentally with effect from 1 April 1996, when it was placed on a statutory footing following the Criminal Injuries Compensation Act 1995. The new scheme broke the link with common law damages. It moved away from payment based on individual assessment, and provided for payment to be made on the basis of a tariff (or scale) of awards that grouped together injuries of comparable severity and allocated a financial value to them. This value was based on awards made previously by the Criminal Injuries Compensation Board. There are some 330 injury descriptions in the tariff ranked against 25 levels (or bands) of award, ranging from £1,000 to £250,000.

---

35. Details are given in the leaflet 'Victims of Crimes of Violence – a guide to the Criminal Injuries Compensation Scheme' which is available from the police or the Criminal Injuries Compensation Authority.

7   Crime reduction strategy

7.1   The Crime Reduction Programme (CRP)

A new Crime Reduction Programme (CRP) for England and Wales was announced in July 1998. The CRP is an evidence-based approach to reducing crime. Resources are being invested in projects that offer a significant and sustained impact on crime. The programme is intended to contribute to reversing the long term growth rate in crime by ensuring the greatest impact for the money spent. The Crime Reduction Programme covers five broad themes:

- working with families, children and schools to prevent young people becoming the offenders of the future
- tackling crime in communities, particularly high volume crime such as domestic burglary
- developing products and systems which are more resistant to crime
- more effective sentencing practices
- working with offenders to ensure that they do not reoffend.

Initiatives found to be most cost-effective in tackling crime and its causes will form the basis of future crime reduction initiatives. Initiatives already underway include burglary reduction, targeted policing, tackling school exclusions, the installation of CCTV systems in high-crime areas, improving the information available to sentencers and tackling domestic violence.

7.2   Crime and disorder partnerships and strategies

A partnership approach to tackling crime and disorder was set in place by the Crime and Disorder Act 1998, in recognition that organisations and individuals working together can achieve more than if they work in isolation. The Crime and Disorder Act 1998 places a joint responsibility upon local authorities and police to formulate and implement strategies to reduce crime and disorder in their area. They must do this in co-operation with a large number of other organisations from the statutory, private and voluntary sectors. They must also consult the local community about their proposals. The first strategies under this legislation were in place by 1 April 1999, initially for three years, and contain clear objectives and performance targets so that progress can be monitored. In addition, these partnerships are required to set five year targets for the reduction of crime (see 7.3).

Figure 7.1: An example of a possible local Crime and Disorder Reduction Partnership

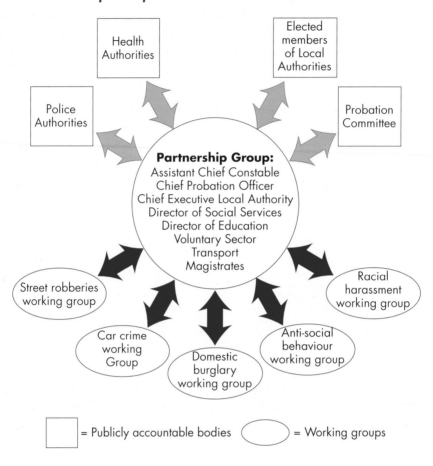

There is no typical partnership as the structure varies considerably from area to area, as do the agencies involved and the seniority of representatives. However, Figure 7.1 shows what a Crime and Disorder reduction partnership might look like.

Partnership groups make decisions concerning the setting of local priorities, targets, strategies and resources. Most partnership groups have established a series of working groups to assist this process. The working groups bring particular expertise to bear on a specific issue and make recommendations. Membership of the working groups will vary in terms of the issues that they are concerned with. Working groups may contain a wider range of agencies than those represented in the Partnership group including such agencies as Victim Support, and neighbourhood watch schemes.

7.3   Crime targets

From April 2000 Crime and Disorder Reduction Partnerships and police authorities have been required to set five-year targets for the reduction of burglary, vehicle crime and robbery. If the targets are achieved they will account nationally for a 30 per cent fall in vehicle crime and a 26 per cent reduction in domestic burglary.

By 2001, the plans to achieve these targets will be scrutinised and monitored in all areas by Her Majesty's Inspectorate of Constabulary and the Audit Commission, in collaboration with Regional Crime Reduction Directors, who will be based in each of the Government's regional offices. These inspections will monitor the performance of partnerships against their agreed strategies and the integration of their work with other government strategies both locally and nationally.

7.4   Crime Reduction Task Force

The Crime Reduction Task Force includes members of police forces and representatives of local and central government. The role of the Task Force is to support the local Crime and Disorder partnerships and Regional Crime Reduction Directors by providing a national focus for the partnerships and giving advice and guidance. This may include guidance on target setting, how to involve different agencies, and the development of good practice.

7.5   Crime Concern

Crime Concern was set up by the Government in 1988 as an independent crime prevention organisation to stimulate the development and dissemination of best practice in crime prevention activity across the professional and voluntary fields. Funding is obtained through business sponsorship and the organisation also receives funding from the Home Office.

Crime Concern works closely with the Home Office on a range of crime reduction issues. As part of specific projects, it currently:

- provides support for the Crime Reduction Partnerships set up under the Crime and Disorder Act 1998
- supports the reducing burglary initiatives
- advises Youth Offending Teams and partnerships in restorative justice
- is involved in extending Youth Action Groups through Youth Action Plus and Primary Action Groups (the latter with the Retail Crime Reduction Action Team)
- works on pilot projects for the Neighbourhood Safety Programme.

8.   Current statistical trends

Table 8A: *Key Indicators from the Criminal Justice System in England & Wales 1988–1998*

	1988	1993	1996	1997	1998
Policing and Crime					
Notifiable offences recorded by the police (millions)[1]	3.72	5.53	5.04	4.60	5.11[2]
Percentage of recorded offences cleared up by the police	35	25	26	28	29
Offenders and Sentences					
(For Indictable Offences only)					
No. of persons found guilty or cautioned (thousands) Total	524	516	490	508	532
aged 10–17	153	130	124	120	127
aged 18–20	94	91	82	86	91
aged 21 and over	277	295	284	302	315
Percentage of offenders sentenced given fines	39	34	28	28	28
Percentage given community penalties[3]	21	26	29	28	28
Percentage given custodial sentences[4]	17	15	22	22	23
The Prison Population					
Average prison population (thousands) Total	50	45	55	61	65
Unsentenced (remand)	11	11	12	12	13
Sentenced	38	33	43	48	52
Non criminal	.2	.6	.6	.6	.5
Average length of prison sentence (in months, for males 21 and over at Crown Court)	19.0	21.8	23.6	24.2	23.6

1. Figures for notifiable offences are based on financial years (1988/89, 93/94, 96/97, 97/98 and 98/99).
2. April 1998 to March 1999. From April 1998, revised counting rules came into effect, meaning the police now count more crimes. This at least partially accounts for the increase seen here – the figure for 1998/99 based on the old counting rules is 4.48 million.
3. Probation orders, supervision orders, community service orders, attendance centre orders, combination orders and curfew orders.
4. Custodial sentences here include unsuspended imprisonment, detention under s.53 of the Children & Young Persons Act 1933, secure training orders and detention in a Young Offenders Institute.

A: Offences recorded by the police

In 1999/2000, the police recorded 5.3 million crimes. Eighty-three per cent of these were against property, 13 per cent were violent and the remaining four per cent were other types of crime.

The number of recorded crimes rose by 3.8 per cent from the previous twelve months. The figures in 1999/2000 and 1998/9 have been effected by changes in the counting rules and coverage of offences used when recording incidents. Comparisons with previous years in this section have been made on the basis of the old counting rules.

Recorded crime fell for five consecutive years from 1992/3 to 1997/8, before the recent rises. Despite this fall, the underlying trend since 1989/90 has been predominantly upwards.

Figure 8.1: Notifiable offences recorded by the Police (12 months ending March 2000)

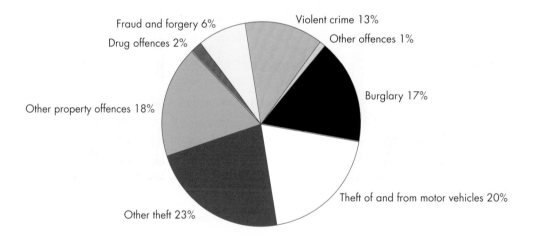

Figure 8.1 shows the breakdown of recorded crime by offence type. Offences of theft account for almost half of recorded crimes. The most frequent types of theft are theft of or from motor vehicles, which account for about a fifth of all recorded offences. Burglary, mainly involving property of small value, accounts for another 17 per cent of recorded crime. Fraud and forgery made up six per cent of recorded crime in 1999/2000. A large proportion of these are cheque and credit card frauds - 173,857 offences in 1999/2000.

There were 703,105 violent crimes recorded in 1999/2000. Of these, 83 per cent were violence against the person – which covers a range of offences including murder, wounding and common assault. The majority of these (95 per cent) incidents were not life-threatening – such as possession of weapons, cruelty to children and common assault.

In 1999/2000, 25 per cent of crimes were cleared up by the police, falling from 29 per cent the previous year. 'Clearing up' a crime means that the police consider that they have identified the offender. For the crimes cleared up in 1999/2000, 57 per cent resulted in a person being charged or summoned for an offence and 17 per cent in a caution. A further 17 per cent resulted in no further action, and 8 per cent were taken into consideration when an individual was charged with other offences.

Figure 8.2:   Recorded crimes and clear-ups

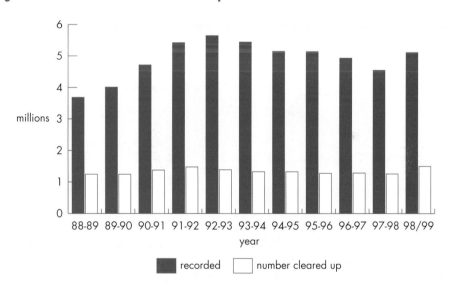

B: The British Crime Survey

The recorded crime statistics only include those offences (mainly indictable) recorded by the police. The 1998 British Crime Survey, based upon interviews with adults living in private households, estimates that, for offence categories that can be compared with those recorded by the police, the true level of crime is about four times higher than that recorded by the police. This is because many offences are not reported to the police, and not all those that are reported are recorded.

The main reasons victims give for not reporting offences to the police are that:

- they do not consider the incident serious enough (44%)
- the police would not be able to do much (33%)
- the police would not be interested (22%)
- victims wanted to deal with it themselves (11%).

The disparity between the recorded figures and the estimates given by the BCS varies according to offence type. For example, for thefts of vehicles BCS and police recorded figures are relatively similar, because victims more readily report such thefts to the police in order to obtain help in recovering their vehicles and for insurance purposes.

Over the period 1987–1997, for those crimes that can be compared, recorded crime increased by 18 per cent. The BCS shows a slightly greater rise of 20 per cent. Despite these increases, both measures showed falls between 1995 and 1997: recorded crime fell by 12 per cent and BCS crime fell by 15 per cent. The BCS is to be an annual survey from 2001.

Figure 8.3:   Recorded, reported and not reported crime for different offence types

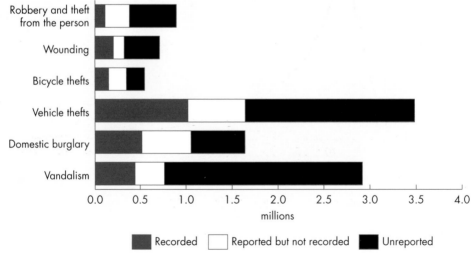

C: Offenders

The peak age for known offending was 18 for males and 15 for females in 1998. This is based on offenders cautioned by the police or convicted by the courts for indictable offences relative to the population. Males made up 82 per cent of those convicted or cautioned for all offences in 1998. Forty-one per cent of known offenders (indictable offences only) were aged under 21 in 1998.

In 1998, of those known offenders committing indictable offences, 61 per cent of juvenile offenders (those aged 10 to 17) were cautioned, 35 per cent of those aged 18 to 20 and 26 per cent of those aged 21 or over were cautioned. The proportion of offenders cautioned has remained relatively stable since the mid 1990s. Prior to this there was a sharp rise, which was halted by a Home Office circular in 1994 which discouraged both multiple cautions and the use of cautions for the most serious offences.

Figure 8.4:   *Age of convicted or cautioned offenders by gender for indictable offences, 1998*

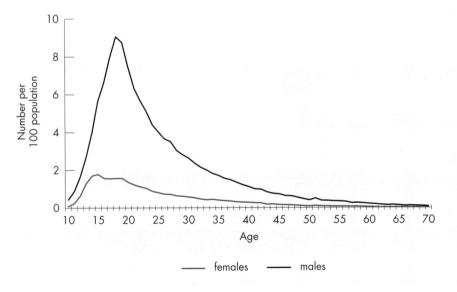

D: Sentencing

Figure 8.5:   Sentencing trends for indictable offences

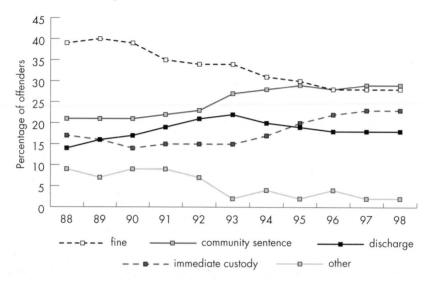

Custody

The number of offenders sentenced to immediate custody for all offences was 100,600 in 1998. This number has increased by 71 per cent since 1993. Prior to 1993, use of immediate custody had fallen. The increase in the mid to late 1990s was seen in both magistrates' courts and the Crown Court, for both summary and indictable offences and for all age groups of offenders. Twenty-three per cent of those sentenced for an indictable offence received a custodial sentence in 1998.

There was a steady increase in sentence lengths for all imprisoned offenders between 1988 and 1997. This was particularly marked for more serious offences such as violence, sexual offences, burglary and robbery. However, for most offences the average sentence length has fallen again between 1997 and 1998.

Figure 8.6:   *Percentage use of immediate custody for selected offences, 1998*

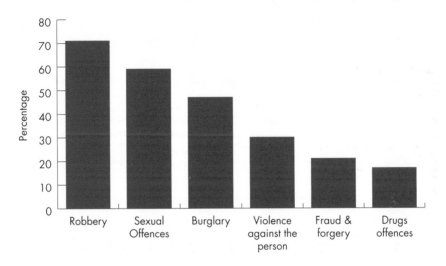

For adult males at magistrates' courts, the average sentence length for indictable offences was 2.6 months in 1998, whereas at the Crown Court the average was 23.6 months. For burglary at the Crown Court, the average length of sentence was 22 months in 1998, for robbery 47 months and for drug offences 32 months.

Fines

The fine is the most commonly used disposal. In 1998, 28 per cent of offenders sentenced for indictable offences received a fine as the primary sentence. The figure for summary non-motoring offences was 80 per cent, and for summary motoring offences, 90 per cent. The use of fines has been declining steadily in recent years. In 1988, 39 per cent of those sentenced for indictable offences received a fine.

Other non-custodial measures

For those sentenced for indictable offences in 1998, 18 per cent were given an absolute or conditional discharge, 28 per cent were given a community sentence: nine per cent received a community service order, 11 per cent a probation order and four per cent a combination order. The percentage of offenders receiving community sentences has remained stable since the early 1990s.

E: Prison Population

The prison population of England and Wales fell from a high of 49,900 in 1988 to 45,700 in 1990, after which it remained relatively constant until 1993. After this, the average number of people in prison rose steadily to 65,300 in 1998. A maximum of 66,500 was reached in July 1998. At the end of March 2000, the prison population was 65,460. This was 2,230 greater than the Certified Normal Accommodation – the number of places prisons officially have available, which was 63,230.

Figure 8.7:   Average criminal prison population 1989 – 1999

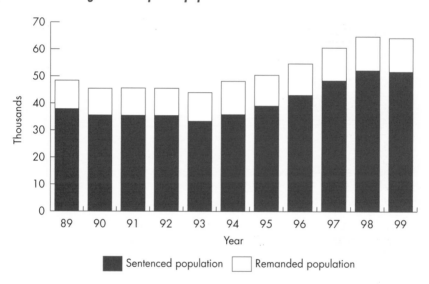

In 1999, sentenced prisoners made up 80 per cent of the prison population. Nineteen per cent were being held on remand (either untried or awaiting sentence). Non-criminal prisoners (the majority of which are held under the 1971 Immigration Act) made up the remaining one per cent.

Five per cent of the prison population in England and Wales were female in 1999. There were about 8,000 sentenced young male offenders, and just over 300 sentenced young female offenders in custody in 1999. These young people, most of whom are under 21, constitute 13 per cent of the total prison population.

Foreign nationals made up 7.5 per cent of the sentenced prison population in 1999. Among British nationals 14 per cent of sentenced prisoners were from minority ethnic groups. This compares with five per cent in the population as a whole (for males aged 15 to 64 and females aged 15 to 54).

In England and Wales in 1999, the rate of imprisonment (the number of people in prison per 100,000 population) was 125. This compares with 118 in Scotland, 89 in France, 109 in Canada and 682 in the US.

Figure 8.8:   Prison Population per 100,000 population for selected countries, 1999

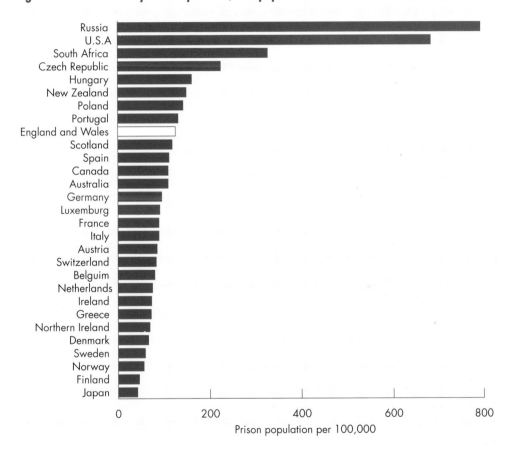

Further information

Annual reports
The following are the main annual publications which relate to the CJS:

- Home Office Annual Report (The Stationery Office Limited)
- Crown Prosecution Service Annual Report (The Stationery Office Limited)
- Lord Chancellor's Department Annual Report (The Stationery Office Limited)
- The Court Service Annual Report (The Stationery Office Limited)
- Report of Her Majesty's Chief Inspector of Constabulary (The Stationery Office Limited)
- Report of Her Majesty's Chief Inspector of Prisons (The Stationery Office Limited)
- Report of Her Majesty's Magistrates' Courts Service Inspectorate (The Stationery Office Limited)
- Report of the Parole Board (The Stationery Office Limited)
- Prison Service Report and Accounts (The Stationery Office Limited)
- Report of the Criminal Injuries Compensation Board (The Stationery Office Limited)
- The Criminal Justice System Business Plan.

Additional statistical reports
The following are regular statistical reports relating to the CJS:

- Criminal statistics, England and Wales (The Stationery Office Limited)
- Judicial statistics, England and Wales (The Stationery Office Limited)
- Prison statistics, England and Wales (The Stationery Office Limited)
- Probation statistics, England and Wales (Home Office)
- Statistics on Women and the Criminal Justice System. A Home Office publication under section 95 of the Criminal Justice Act 1991 (Home Office)
- Statistics on Race and the Criminal Justice System. A Home Office publication under section 95 of the Criminal Justice Act 1991 (Home Office)
- Digest – Information on the Criminal Justice System in England and Wales (Home Office) (not annual, but periodic)
- Public Expenditure: Statistical Analyses, HM Treasury (The Stationery Office Limited).

Requests for publications

Home Office Statistical Bulletins, Home Office Research Studies, Research Findings and Occasional Papers can be downloaded from the RDS website at
http://www.homeoffice.gov.uk/rds/index.htm
where an up-to-date list of publications is also available.

Paper copies of publications can be obtained from:
> RDS Communication and Development Unit
> Room 201
> 50 Queen Anne's Gate
> London SW1H 9AT
> Tel: 020 7273 2084
> Fax: 020 7222 0211
> E-mail: publications.rds@homeoffice.gsi.gov.uk

Stationery Office publications are available from:
> The Stationery Office Limited
> The Publications Centre
> PO Box 276
> London SW8 5DT
> General enquiries: 020 7873 0011
> Fax orders: 020 7873 8200
> Website: http://www.the-stationery-office.co.uk

The 2000 Criminal Justice System Business Plan is available at:
> http://www.criminal-justice-system.gov.uk

The Digest is available at:
> http://www.homeoffice.gov.uk/rds/index.htm

Useful website addresses

Court Service:	http://www.courtservice.gov.uk
Crime Reduction:	http://www.crimereduction.gov.uk
Criminal Cases Review Commission:	http://www.ccrc.gov.uk
Criminal Courts Review:	http://www.criminal-courts-review.org.uk
Criminal Justice System:	http://www.criminal-justice-system.gov.uk
Crown Prosecution Service:	http://www.cps.gov.uk
HM Inspector of Constabulary:	http://www.homeoffice.gov.uk/hmic/hmic.htm
HM Inspectorate of Prisons:	http://www.homeoffice.gov.uk/hmipris/hmipris.htm
HM Inspectorate of Probation:	http://www.homeoffice.gov.uk/hmiprob/hmiprob.htm
HM Magistrates' Court Inspectorate:	http://www.open.gov.uk/mcsi
Home Office:	http://www.homeoffice.gov.uk
Judicial Studies Board:	http://www.cix.co.uk/~jsb/index.htm
Just Ask:	http://www.justask.org.uk/
The Law Commission:	http://www.gtnet.gov.uk/lawcomm/homepage.htm
The Law Society:	http://www.lawsociety.org.uk/Index.asp
Legal Aid Board:	http://www.legal-aid.gov.uk
Legal Services:	http://www.legalservices.gov.uk
Lexicon:	http://www.courtservice.gov.uk/lexicon/index.htm
Lord Chancellor's Department:	http://www.open.gov.uk/lcd
Magistrates Association:	http://www.magistrates-association.org.uk
Magistrates' Court Service:	http://www.open.gov.uk/lcd/magist/magistfr.htm
Open Government:	http://www.open.gov.uk
Police Services of the UK:	http://www.police.uk
Prison Service:	http://www.hmprisonservice.gov.uk
Probation Service:	http://www.homeoffice.gov.uk/new_indexs/index_probation.htm
UK Official Publications:	http://www.official-documents.co.uk/menu/ukpinf.htm
UK Parliament:	http://www.parliament.uk/
Victim Support:	http://www.victimsupport.com
Youth Justice Board:	http://www.youth-justice-board.gov.uk